Educator
Bandwidth

ASCD MEMBER BOOK

Many ASCD members received this book as a
member benefit upon its initial release.

Learn more at: **www.ascd.org/memberbooks**

Jane A.G. Kise • Ann C. Holm

Educator Bandwidth

How to Reclaim
Your Energy, Passion, and Time

ascd

Arlington, Virginia USA

2800 Shirlington Rd., Ste. 1001 • Arlington, VA 22206
Phone: 800-933-2723 or 703-578-9600 • Fax: 703-575-5400
Website: www.ascd.org • Email: member@ascd.org
Author guidelines: www.ascd.org/write

Penny Reinart, *Chief Impact Officer;* Genny Ostertag, *Managing Director, Book Acquisitions & Editing;* Susan Hills, *Senior Acquisitions Editor;* Julie Houtz, *Director, Book Editing;* Megan Doyle, *Editor;* Thomas Lytle, *Creative Director;* Donald Ely, *Art Director;* Georgia Park, *Senior Graphic Designer;* Cynthia Stock, *Typesetter;* Kelly Marshall, *Production Manager;* Shajuan Martin, *E-Publishing Specialist;* Christopher Logan, *Senior Production Specialist*

PAPERBACK ISBN: 978-1-4166-3113-2   ASCD product #122019
PDF E-BOOK ISBN: 978-1-4166-3114-9; see Books in Print for other formats.
Quantity discounts are available: email programteam@ascd.org or call 800-933-2723, ext. 5773, or 703-575-5773. For desk copies, go to www.ascd.org/deskcopy.

ASCD Member Book No. FY22-8 (Jul. 2022 PSI+). ASCD Member Books mail to Premium (P), Select (S), and Institutional Plus (I+) members on this schedule: Jan, PSI+; Feb, P; Apr, PSI+; May, P; Jul, PSI+; Aug, P; Sep, PSI+; Nov, PSI+; Dec, P. For current details on membership, see www.ascd.org/membership.

Library of Congress Cataloging-in-Publication Data

Names: Kise, Jane A. G., author. | Holm, Ann, author.
Title: Educator bandwidth : how to reclaim your energy, passion, and time / Jane A. G. Kise and Ann Holm.
Description: Arlington, Virginia USA : ASCD, [2022] | Includes bibliographical references and index.
Identifiers: LCCN 2022003030 (print) | LCCN 2022003031 (ebook) | ISBN 9781416631132 (paperback) | ISBN 9781416631149 (pdf)
Subjects: LCSH: Teachers—Job stress—Prevention. | Teachers—Psychology. | Teachers—Mental health.
Classification: LCC LB2840.2 .K58 2022 (print) | LCC LB2840.2 (ebook) | DDC 371.1001/9—dc23
LC record available at https://lccn.loc.gov/2022003030
LC ebook record available at https://lccn.loc.gov/2022003031

31 30 29 28 27 26 25 24 23 22   1 2 3 4 5 6 7 8 9 10 11 12

To the teachers who dedicated a significant amount of bandwidth to nurturing and educating my own children—especially Sue Haugerud, Kevin Bjerken, Wendy Shearer, Mark DeYoung, Mary Erani, Scott Charlesworth-Seiler, David Henderson, and their dear Montessori teachers Mrs. Lali and Mrs. Jayantha.

—Jane A. G. Kise

For my daughter Natalie Ann Espe, a dedicated high school social studies teacher, and to her grandmother Wilma Holm, an 8th grade teacher who first sparked Natalie's interest in the noble calling of teaching.

—Ann C. Holm

Educator Bandwidth

How to Reclaim Your Energy, Passion, and Time

1

Why Bandwidth? Why Now?

Curiosity Creator

Which of these are your biggest wishes?

- I wish I had more time to just be!
- I wish no one but my closest friends had my mobile phone number!
- I wish someone else would decide what we're having for dinner!
- I wish my children/students had no interest in screen time!
- I wish I could sit back with a good book (or a guitar or an art project or simply to think) and not get distracted!
- I wish I wasn't so busy all the time!

All of these are connected with your supply of brain energy and bandwidth, which we'll explain in a moment, and whether they are sufficient. When you think of brain energy and bandwidth, what comes to mind? What factors indicate your mind is overtaxed and underfueled? At first glance, what needs to change to restore your sense of optimal functioning?

Why Bandwidth?

Did you ever have one of those groups of students? You know, you're using the same surefire lessons and materials, and it isn't working with this particular group? You start wondering, "It has to be them. This never fails. What is it with these kids?"

Ann and I experienced this big-time with an education organization we'd worked with for years. Serving as external coaches for their intensive and lengthy aspiring leadership program, we'd successfully guided three cohorts through self-discovery assessments, 360 feedback, and goal setting. But what about this fourth group?

Unlike the previous cohorts, these leaders were struggling to keep their coaching appointments and complete assessments. Further, collecting 360 feedback from their supervisors, sponsors, and peers was positively torturous. "We need more time!" they pleaded.

Jane, preparing to keynote at a banquet for the participants, their sponsors, and other leaders in the organization, asked Ann, "What if I give a quiz to jump-start their awareness of the busy-ness trap they've fallen into?" We drafted 15 questions, a first run at what became our Brain Energy and Bandwidth Survey, using the latest neuroscience research on habits that enhance and derail executive function.

At the banquet, Jane read the questions aloud, asking participants to give themselves a 0, 2, or 4 on each item. Groans, chuckles, and comments such as "In what universe could that happen?" echoed around the room. Out of a possible 60 points (we assumed that anyone below 30 was probably experiencing stress from various competing priorities), many participants scored as low as 10.

More significant is what happened next during their two-day seminar. Bandwidth was almost the only topic, no matter what subject the facilitators introduced. We received text and email pleas for help from the people we coached. "I've got to change my habits and increase my score." "No wonder I'm exhausted." "I wasn't even noticing how crazy my calendar was until I answered those questions." "Help! You're right! How I'm working isn't working!"

We helped them—and then other clients and colleagues around the world—pinpoint which practices were draining their energy and how to become more effective, efficient, and engaged—and more contented—with the priorities they set. We welcomed help from colleague Dr. Greg Huszczo to validate results, identify predictive items, and use factor analysis to revise and group the items into the survey you can take as a reader of this book.

Our hope is that these pages will help educators

- Identify their top priorities in life.
- Define for themselves what it means to honor those priorities.
- Make the most of what neuroscience has revealed about the keys to your energy, passion, and time.
- Influence organizations to develop norms, policies, and leadership modeling of the practices and habits that allow each individual to maximize their bandwidth.

We're going to ask you to stop thinking about finding more time and instead start working toward contentment with how you spend your time. Think about it. We've all had 24 hours in a day since the geniuses of ancient civilizations figured out how long it took for the Earth to complete a rotation. No one has more than 24 hours in a day. No one has less. The truth is no one has more *time*. This book isn't about trying to cram more things into an already crazy schedule, but rather it's about aligning how you use your time with what is important to you and for your brain.

You can't do it all, at least not all at the same time. One of the key research-based points we'll be making is that understanding what your brain truly needs allows you to follow through on the priorities you set so that you are truly contented. We call this having enough *bandwidth*.

What Is Bandwidth?

So, what is bandwidth? Think of it as the energy that powers the brain's prefrontal cortex—the center of executive function. This small area of the brain uses a tremendous amount of energy as we work to make good decisions, focus on cognitively demanding tasks, be patient and empathetic, and engage in necessary self-care such as eating well. While these seem like completely separate activities, they all draw on the same limited pool of brain energy. In some way, they also all draw on willpower.

Baumeister and Tierney (2011) cite numerous experiments illustrating how using energy for any of these activities leaves us vulnerable to lapses in willpower, and one studied how concentrating on solving complex problems affected snacking. Participants assigned to difficult cognitive tasks consumed more sweets than those who spent the same amount of time reading for pleasure. This second group contentedly munched on salad fixings such as radishes even though they were also offered sweets. The researchers summarize as follows.

1. You have a finite amount of willpower that becomes depleted as you use it. 2. You use the same stock of willpower for all manner of tasks. You might think you have one reservoir of self-control for work, another for dieting, another for exercise, and another for being nice to your family. But the radish experiment showed that two completely unrelated activities—resisting chocolate and working on geometry puzzles—drew on the same source of energy, and this phenomenon has been demonstrated over and over. . . . There are hidden connections among the wildly different things you do all day.

You use the same supply of willpower to deal with frustrating traffic, tempting food, annoying colleagues, demanding bosses, pouting children. Resisting dessert at lunch leaves you with less willpower to praise your boss' awful haircut. (p. 35)

You can increase the amount of bandwidth you have using specific behaviors, similar to how you can increase your car's fuel capacity by installing a bigger fuel tank. However, use up bandwidth for one of the above functions and you'll be running on empty for the others. Long before you feel the kind of fatigue associated with burnout, you're depleting the energy you need to be effective, efficient, emotionally intelligent, and engaged in your work (McGonigal, 2011).

Chapter by chapter, we'll guide you through the steps to identify how well you're handling the factors that increase your bandwidth *and* how to choose actions that will help you find a balance between work life and personal life that brings contentment.

In 2018, we began customizing the content for K–12 educators. And then? The COVID-19 pandemic hit.

Why Work on Bandwidth Now?

Even before the pandemic, teaching consistently ranked as one of the most stressful professions in the world (Busby, 2019). Since March 2020, teacher stress has only increased (Cipriano & Brackett, 2020). We'll cover how stress interferes with brain energy and bandwidth, but we know from our research that the number one predictor that an individual's score will fall into the healthy range on our survey is whether that person feels their workplace culture and policies support good bandwidth.

This means that schools need to very seriously address the factors that lead to good bandwidth. When leaders say, "But we have so many other priorities," we point out that low bandwidth scores mean people are *losing their ability to be energized, effective, efficient, engaged, and emotionally intelligent.* Low educator bandwidth interferes with the immensely difficult mission to help every student reach full potential.

Here are four other core reasons to dig into improving bandwidth now.

First, **we only tend to pay attention to what we measure**—and measuring bandwidth can be key to understanding how effective each of us can be. Margaret Wheatley and Myron Kellner-Rogers (1999) suggest we develop measures that let us know whether we are increasing capacities critical to carrying out the organizational mission. Bandwidth falls into this category.

Second, **adults can't guide students in social and emotional learning** if the adults are burned out, disengaged, and ineffective! Research supports this, but instead of reading about it, try engaging in a gedanken (thought) experiment.

> Sit comfortably, close your eyes, and imagine yourself arriving at your classroom after a restless night's sleep, worried about an argument with your child over homework or with a friend over a hot issue, hungry because you forgot to grab that protein bar after that argument. Where is your energy level as students enter the room?
>
> Now imagine yourself after a good night's sleep. You munch that bar, placed in your bag the night before, as you open the folder with the day's work all set to go. There weren't any arguments last night about homework because your teen knows that you'll schedule their studying every evening if you get a notice from the school portal that grades are slipping. Where is your energy level now?

Einstein is credited with formalizing the use of these conceptual rather than physical experiments—and they are underused in education. For example, do we need research to confirm that 6-year-olds whose school days include breaks for physical activity and socialization can concentrate more fully on learning as required? Or, through a gedanken experiment, can you envision yourself as a 6-year-old, asked to sit still for an hour (or an adult asked to sit still for a full 60 minutes of professional development)? How long would it be before you started fidgeting? Einstein *couldn't* physically experiment with traveling at the speed of light, yet he developed the theory of relativity. Similarly, we can used informed gedanken experiments to draw sound conclusions in commonsense areas to improve outcomes for students.

This is a simple example. Remember, if you use up your bandwidth for one area, such as worry, or if you don't fuel up in the first place, you have less bandwidth available to model the patience and kindness and resilience we are trying to foster in students.

Third, **because the digital age has hijacked the brains of billions of people** without their conscious awareness, few individuals, and even fewer organizations, have adjusted to dampen the impact and implications. Not long ago, sending a message took time. You had to find a pen and paper, or secure a typewriter, and with luck, didn't have to revise your message. You were also reasonably assured that your message would reach only its intended recipient and wouldn't be widely shared. The idea that a message could be sent around the world in milliseconds and that it could "go viral" was the stuff of science fiction books.

Then the digital age seemingly exploded out of nowhere with the introduction of smartphones in 2007. This new era arrived absent any guidelines, strategies, or manuals. Suddenly we were immersed in it, and the rules evolved organically, largely driven by newly formed habits that were not deliberate but reactive. More on that later. Our corporate and executive clients began to report stories like these:

> "We had hoped that decreasing the need to travel by going virtual would save everyone time. Instead we ended up having to attend more meetings."

> "Whatever happened to lunch? That time is now spent returning emails while we mindlessly eat whatever is available."

> "Even simple, low-risk decisions are researched endlessly on the internet. What should take moments to decide is drawn out well beyond what makes sense."

> "I am working until midnight. What happened to the promise of the 30-hour work week technology would bring us?"

No, this wasn't the intended outcome of the digital age. While the 2020 pandemic may have provided a few unexpected perks as we worked remotely, such as more time to manage meals and less time commuting, think of the original promises of computers and the internet. Everything was supposed to get easier, and we were going to get more done in less time with fewer resources. Computers would take over the boring, repetitive tasks. Instead, the digital age has stretched us to the point where we can't seem to keep up—we get more emails, more data, more information, more meetings scheduled on those virtual calendars, with no more time to do it all. Humans aren't machines; the relationship between productivity and time on task isn't linear.

Fourth, **compounding the effects of digital data and connectivity in education are deep-seated norms.** For example, research shows that teachers do not feel empowered to engage in self-care practices, a crucial part of bandwidth, unless leaders model it (Skakon et al., 2010). Further, we can't keep saying, "That's just the way it is," or, "We simply have to do more with less," or, "Professionals put their students first." There is individual and organization responsibility to make the changes that improve bandwidth. If we're going to change the way we're working to once again honor the way our brains have evolved over millennia, organizational attention to bandwidth is essential.

How to Use This Book

Hopefully, this chapter has demonstrated the importance of ensuring you have enough brain energy and bandwidth to reclaim your energy, passion, and time.

Your next step is to take the Brain Energy and Bandwidth Survey. Chapter 2 will guide you through interpreting your results and choosing the one or two areas for focus that are most important in your current circumstances.

Chapter 3 describes how habits form and the most effective strategies for changing unhelpful habits. For example, committing to something (e.g., "I will read those books I've been dying to get to") rather than quitting something (e.g., "I won't watch television") produces far more success. Reaching rather than resisting uses far less willpower, freeing up that limited willpower for other things!

Chapter 4 lets you think about the policies, cultural norms, and espoused beliefs in your learning community that affect individual bandwidth. We often hear from teachers and other employees "But I can't change policies over what meetings I have to be at or when I start my day." And, leaders tell us, "But I can't change people's sleep and diet habits." That chapter will name and explore this tension, mapping out how to stop focusing on what you can't control to gain clarity around what action steps are in your sphere of influence.

Chapters 5–10 expand the information on the six areas covered by the Brain Energy and Bandwidth survey. You'll find information on the neuroscience behind the survey items, examples of individuals and organizations that have improved how they handle each area, and solid suggestions for forming habits that will increase your bandwidth.

Finally, Chapter 11 tackles organizational support of bandwidth. Through a case study and suggested planning process, we will illustrate the power of using data to change the conversation from "this is the way things have to be" to "we have to change things; let's figure it out!"

Forming a Bandwidth Band

Each chapter ends with questions that guide you through how to set an action plan to improve your bandwidth and some group discussion questions.

We highly encourage forming a "Bandwidth Band" and tackling the chapters together week by week, not all at once. Consider joining with at least three other educators to discuss the book, commit to action steps, and support each other in improving your bandwidth. Why?

- Researchers have demonstrated that each of us constructs knowledge as we learn, and deeper, broader learning happens while engaged with a diverse group of other learners (Black & Allen, 2018).
- While some people are more attracted to accountability groups and some to support groups, the truth is, with the kind of guidance this book provides, your group can function in both of these ways, helping you set reasonable goals, reminding you to celebrate small wins, and supplying encouragement to fuel your motivation.
- We learn not from experience but from reflecting on experience. Group time builds that reflective time into your schedule—see Chapter

5 on the power of one-off choices that automate activities you know you need but often fall by the wayside in day-to-day busy-ness.

- A group will help you go slow to go fast. We hope this book is engaging enough to keep you reading, but we also hope you won't speed-read and say, "That was fascinating. I really should improve my bandwidth. Now, what's next on my reading list?" (Note: If you've been struggling to focus on texts that require concentration, you might take a peek at Chapter 7, Focus Through Mental Habits.)

Blameless Discernment Moment

One of the core tools in these pages is *blameless discernment*. We don't want our readers feeling shame, guilt, or helplessness—or self-righteousness—about their current level of bandwidth. Shirzad Chamine (2012) provides a handy framework for recognizing when you are blaming or judging instead of discerning how to move forward. While we all occasionally fall into the three traps below, explore the related reflection exercises to discern which might trip you up the most: blaming yourself, blaming others, or blaming circumstances.

Some people tend to over-assign blame to their own actions with thoughts such as "I've tried. I just don't have willpower." The key to lessening these judgments is focusing your ability to empathize on yourself. Try this reflection:

> Bring to mind a picture of yourself as a small child under the age of 10. Find a real picture if it helps. Now, think of the empathy and grace you deserved at this tender age. You deserved love, understanding, and second chances. Turn that same empathy toward your adult self. You deserve more bandwidth as you strive to become your most authentic self. Imagine giving yourself grace and compassion as you identify what you are doing well. Picture supporting yourself much like a caring adult guides the back of a bicycle while a new rider learns to pedal—watchful, encouraging, supportive.

Some people tend to over-assign blame to others with thoughts such as "How can I possibly increase bandwidth with all the demands our leaders make of us?" The key to blameless discernment is directing empathy toward those who seem to swallow up your bandwidth. Try this reflection:

Imagine yourself in the shoes of this leader, colleague, or family member. What might be driving them to create such an atmosphere or make such demands? Try speaking in the first person. For example, you might imagine yourself as the superintendent who just imposed yet another reporting requirement. If asked, that person might say something like "The buck stops on my desk, along with a thousand other expectations from the school board. I need proof of all we're doing."

Some people tend to over-assign blame to circumstances with thoughts such as "As long as I'm a teacher/parent/caregiver/team leader/ stuck in this building, I can't improve my bandwidth." Try the opposite of empathy: objectivity.

Imagine yourself as an objective observer of your circumstances. What might you notice, without judgment, about the facts and assumptions you use to judge circumstances? What truly can and can't be changed? What is and isn't under your control?

The trick isn't to stop judging but to blamelessly discern the role you are playing, how others affect what happened, and other factors and circumstances a curious, objective observer might note. Only then can we pinpoint next steps that will truly improve our brain energy and bandwidth. Again and again in these pages, we'll be asking you to consider your brain energy and bandwidth through this lens of blameless discernment so that you can set aside any guilt, frustration, feelings of entrapment, or concerns that nothing can really change.

Instead, with blameless discernment, join us on this journey to explore how you can use research on the brain, on habit formation, on learning, on social constructs, and more to maximize your brain energy and bandwidth for the things that matter most to you at home and at school.

My initial reaction to my score was "This bandwidth stuff is just another thing to induce guilt on working moms—especially after a pandemic when we had to do it all or risk losing it all." Then upon further reflection, I realized that the pandemic caused me to get really out of balance. In order to survive I did have to do it all, but should it have to be that way forever? I think working parents can benefit from periodically reevaluating how their bandwidth is out of balance and then make changes without feeling guilty. This bandwidth tool is a good way to bring things back in balance: good for spouse, children, and families!

—Early childhood special education teacher, mother of four

Bandwidth Band Discussion Guide

1. Before you begin, agree to your band's logistics.
   - Establish confidentiality.
   - How often will you meet? Ideally, groups meet nine times, discussing the first 10 chapters in the book (combine the discussion of Chapters 1 and 2).
   - Will the same person act as leader for each meeting, or will you rotate this role? The leader guides the group through the suggested discussion questions, works to include everyone in the discussion, and ensures the meeting ends at the agreed-upon time.
   - What expectations does everyone have? Does everyone anticipate being able to read a chapter and complete at least one of the self-reflection exercises? What else?
2. Start your first discussion by sharing what you hope to gain from the bandwidth journey. How will you know you have gotten the outcome you desire?
3. Consider your current ability to engage in blameless discernment. How will blameless discernment affect your outcomes? What type of shift will be necessary to optimize your brain and bandwidth?
4. Reflect together on the "Blameless Discernment Moment" for this chapter. Share examples of how you misattributed blame and how changing that perspective changed your approach to a dilemma. For example, Jane used to blame the circumstance of traffic delays while commuting back and forth to visit her elderly mother for lack of reading time. Then she realized she could recapture that time with audiobooks as she drove. Yes, she was stuck in the car, but she had choices about how to use that time.

2

Your Bandwidth Survey Results

Before you begin reading this chapter, take the Brain Energy and Bandwidth Survey in the Appendix. To take the Brain Energy and Bandwidth Survey online and share it with other educators in your school, visit www.ascd.org/educator-bandwidth-survey.

Curiosity Creator

Which of these statements do you think reflect results from participants in the validation study of the Brain Energy and Bandwidth Survey?[1]

- A. A majority of our survey takers answered "Almost Always" to the item "I attend to emails at set times rather than constantly."
- B. Survey takers who also indicated they prefer to schedule their time scored higher on the "Filtering Through Possibilities" section than did those who reported taking a more spontaneous approach to life.
- C. Women scored higher than men on "Overall Sense of Energy."
- D. GenX and Millennials scored higher on the "Staying Connected" section than Boomers or Elders (born before 1945).
- E. Women scored higher than men on the "Fueling Your Brain" section.

You and Your Brain

The brain is an amazing entity, capable of complex problem solving, planning, adaptability, memory recall, self-regulation, and more. It accounts for 2 percent of our body weight but uses 20 percent of our available energy. When the brain is low on energy, it doesn't operate optimally. Think of each activity that engages your brain as a window on a computer. The more windows you have open, the more you tax the system, often slowing down how fast documents, web pages, and applications load.

Most people feel pretty taxed these days, don't they? Part of this comes from the new demands that technology and societal changes are placing on our brains. Let's walk through what we know about brain evolution, neuroplasticity, and adaptation. The big idea is that human brains slowly evolve over millennia. Individual brains can adapt rather quickly to new demands and even to compensate for injury, but these adaptations aren't always optimal.

Over thousands and thousands of years, our brains evolved for social relationships; these areas of the human brain are far larger than in the primate species most related to humans (Leiberman, 2013).

While human brains seem hardwired for needing these relationships, recent research has generated considerable excitement about the capacity of our brains to change due to neuroplasticity. Just a few decades ago, we thought brains had no capacity to change or rewire. However, in his seminal book, *The Brain That Changes Itself,* Norman Doidge (2007) describes several case studies illustrating the capacity of the brain to form new connections and change. He concluded that all learning involves changing the neural connections in the brain. Still, it's important not to confuse neuroplastic changes, which occur as we interact with our environment and learn, with the evolutionary millennial-spanning changes that occurred to ensure the survival of our species as a whole.

Consider this example of adaptation versus evolution. Infant brains are wired to pick up sounds, recognize voices, and imitate. In an amazingly short time from birth, they say their first words. This capacity evolved over the millennia it took to become the social beings with complex language skills we are. In contrast, only in the past 500 years has access to print increased, creating motivation to master reading. Unlike oral language, humans still need to be taught how to read. *Neuroplasticity*—the brain's ability to rewire and develop no matter how young or old we are—allows humans to build the circuitry needed for reading (Wolf, 2018). However, unlike the capacity we have for learning to speak, there is no one single "reading circuitry" in our brains. Maryanne Wolf discusses the fragility involved in truly mastering reading.

The crux of the matter is that the plasticity of our brain permits us to form both ever more sophisticated and expanded circuits and also ever less sophisticated circuits, depending on environmental factors. (p. 19)

This same plasticity helps us develop brain circuitry for other demands of being modern humans, including using our digital devices, scanning the environment while driving at speeds that our ancestors would view as magical, and more.

But, just as in reading, our brains haven't *evolved*. Even the so-called Digital Native Generation's brains are adapting—and in many cases not adapting in ways that lead to better performance overall. In fact, some habits are maladaptive. They are either inadequate or inappropriate for the task or environment.

This means that we're asking our brains to operate with little consideration for how our brains actually function, leaving us subject to considerable stress and energy depletion. Yes, we have to live in the modern world. However, we need to acknowledge and nurture some of the needs that are simply baked into our DNA.

Thus, most of us find ourselves busier, more distracted, less rested, and less connected in spite of all the promises of the modern world. Our Brain Energy and Bandwidth Survey, based on neuroscience research, is designed to help you understand how well you're balancing brain energy. Simply put, is your "fuel input" sufficient for the demands of your day?

A Good Mindset for the Bandwidth Survey

For your survey results to be as informative as possible, we suggest that you take the survey with the following mindset.

First, adopt the perspective of *blameless discernment*, as discussed in Chapter 1. We've seen that simply answering the questions leads many participants to feel guilty or even helpless.

Instead, please think of the survey as a simple tool, like a thermometer. You're just getting information on your current "temperature." Judging yourself isn't going to help you change. As you notice areas that need to be addressed, refrain from harsh judgments of yourself, others, and circumstances. Brain energy is wasted when we divert it toward negative emotions like despair, anger, and shame. Instead, try to take a step back and look at your brain energy and bandwidth habits through the eyes of a curious observer. The Brain Energy and Bandwidth Survey is merely a tool to help you jump-start that process.

Second, your bandwidth score is a product of the choices you're making *and* your circumstances. Certain seasons of life push our scores lower, even if we wouldn't change those circumstances for anything (such as parenting young children). Recognizing this helps you work with your score with blameless discernment. It's a baseline that lets you identify what actions might be most helpful for you right now. If you are in a particularly challenging season of life, such as providing care for an ill or aging relative or planning a special event or wedding, take that into consideration as you appraise your brain energy and bandwidth. These are special circumstances that might be affecting your overall score on the survey. Be honest about the stress you're experiencing so that you get the most out of the survey. And know that the tips in Chapters 5–10 will help.

Third, be curious. Perhaps as you read some of the items you'll think, "But isn't that just the way it is now?" Know that this book is about making sure you can reclaim your energy, passion, and time. Stomp on helplessness and be ready to step into agency.

Fourth, while the learning community survey discussed in Chapter 11 can provide comparison information as a reference, don't see scores as a competition. This is your baseline. Remember, too, that while some people easily give themselves top scores, others have never given themselves an *A* on anything, always focusing on what they might have done better. If that describes you, your score may be lower than those of others in your Bandwidth Band even if their lives seem crazier than your own.

Pause now and take the survey, if you haven't already, and then read on to understand your score.

Top Eight Items Where Our Control Group Scored Lowest

To keep people from jumping to the conclusion that they are alone in scoring lower than they anticipated on the survey, we've learned to share a list of the lowest-scoring items in our participant database. Which ones do you think they were? The answer is at the end of the chapter in a Bandwidth Band discussion question.

Part of the reason to do this is to consider where unproductive habits come from. As you consider the ones you believe are more of a universal problem, what factors do you think contribute? Why do more people struggle to build what research tells us are productive approaches to these areas of work and life?

The Meaning of Each Bandwidth Survey Score Range

Now let's look at your results.

While our research and analysis confirmed that people with higher scores on the survey report higher levels of energy and engagement with life and work, we can't say for sure the score at which someone does or doesn't have *enough* bandwidth. Far too many factors come into play, including one's "hardiness" (defined in Chapter 4) and comfort level with giving high ratings. Therefore, we use three wide score ranges and describe what most people in those ranges are experiencing.

As you read through these three score ranges, think about each descriptor. Place a check by those that are particularly true for you. Does the description seem accurate as you think about your energy and engagement? If not, were you too hard on yourself or too lenient as you answered the survey? In which score range do your checkmarks cluster? Does it match your score on the survey?

Behaviors associated with the Good Bandwidth range (90–120)
- Managing brain energy input and output well, fueling the brain with proper nutrition, exercise, sleep, and downtime while using strategies to maximize efficiency, such as avoiding multitasking.
- Feeling content with the current balance of work priorities and personal priorities.

- Delegating tasks and responsibilities well.
- Recognizing when brain energy is low and adjusting decision-making behavior accordingly (timing, seeking input, etc.).
- Enjoying work, coworkers, and outside activities most of the time. Engagement level is high.

Behaviors associated with the Mediocre Bandwidth range (60–90)

- Managing some of the energy-creating and energy-draining factors well but would probably see great benefits from improvements in other areas.
- Probably experiencing conflicted feelings about success with properly balancing work and personal goals/interests/responsibilities.
- May be experiencing, or becoming more vulnerable to, health issues because of a lack of adequate sleep, an unhealthy diet, or a sedentary lifestyle.
- Working in a far less efficient manner than they believe they are, accomplishing perhaps 50–70 percent of what someone with a bandwidth score above 90 might do.
- Lacking awareness that their mediocre bandwidth is compromising their ability to make optimal decisions.
- Losing patience with people, things, processes, or circumstances in one or more areas of their lives.

Behaviors associated with the Problematic Bandwidth range (below 60)

- Operating from a "mission critical" stance most of the time.
- Relying on caffeine and other short-term bursts of fuel to revive the brain.
- Leaving multiple issues that require decisions unaddressed.
- Experiencing a type of learned helplessness by feeling constantly interrupted but powerless to do anything about it.
- Demonstrating impatience with others or using avoidance behaviors.
- Feeling burned out or disengaged; may fantasize about quitting their current roles.

Factors That Affect Whether Scores Match Perception

Sometimes a person's score simply doesn't match the descriptors. Here are a few reasons that cause these mismatches.

Passion. If you're really excited by your work, the purpose propelling your busy-ness, or the needs of someone you are caring for, you might be operating on overdrive and not experiencing the Problematic Bandwidth descriptors. Ask yourself, is your current bandwidth sustainable? Might relationships or health or safety give way?

Bandwidth outliers. Some people score really low in only one area, leaving the overall score rather high. Ask yourself, is that one area causing major problems? If so, know that Chapters 5–10, one for each section of the survey, can be read in any sequence if you'd like to start with the one where you scored lowest.

Temporary circumstances. A good example is having an infant in the home. We put up with major fatigue, lack of time for fitness, and less time for our interests because we know the needs of the little human are simply more important. We can run on empty for a while, but use your scores to ponder which area can give you the most bandwidth for the effort needed to make any changes.

Hardiness. The research-based concepts around hardiness have identified a set of strategies for dealing with the inevitable stress of living, loving, and striving for purpose. These can be learned through experience or taught directly. As you'll learn in Chapter 4, people who exhibit hardiness are able to grow from stressful events in their lives. You'll find suggestions for developing more hardiness throughout these pages, but baseline differences in this capacity mean that you might have the exact same bandwidth score as someone else and yet be experiencing a different level of overall energy and engagement.

Overall level of self-awareness. As with any self-reporting tool or questionnaire, our results are affected by our level of self-awareness. Sometimes people are simply not fully aware of what they are doing or the impact of habits and routines. Consider asking a trusted friend, colleague, or family member for their input on your results.

Compare your score to the range descriptions and these common factors for experiencing a mismatch. Bottom line, whether you feel you have enough brain energy and bandwidth is up to you. If you've employed blameless discernment and revisited whether you may have over- or underestimated your current capacity, your final assessment is probably spot-on!

Exploring Brain Energy and Bandwidth Opportunities

Let's turn to what can be done about brain energy and bandwidth. Whatever your score, note that bandwidth is fluid. It isn't something we stabilize once and for all. A change in circumstances—such as a pandemic—affects how we fuel, focus, and filter and what drains our energy. Because of this, we don't want anyone feeling helpless *or* overly confident about their current routines and habits. It won't be productive to try to change too many things at once (more on that in Chapter 3) or to complacently assume you have nothing to worry about. Instead, we ask that you explore Chapters 5–10, one for each of the six areas of bandwidth, with two purposes in mind.

First, explore the neuroscience connections for each area. What might you learn that would increase or decrease the urgency to pay attention to each bandwidth factor? Use these questions to contemplate how this information may be most helpful to you.

- What evidence tells me that I do or do not need to improve my strategies for my mental capacity to be the most effective?
- Which areas are of most concern to me?
- Do I need to check with someone who knows me well to ensure I am focusing on the right areas of concern?

Second, check out each of these chapter's strategies for improving your bandwidth. Sometimes reading about actions you might take changes the urgency of an area. It may increase because you can take a simple step. Or it might decrease because you realize you have bigger fish to fry!

Which ones might you implement right now? If you are a leader, which might be essential for you to model for those you lead? Often, *no one* feels empowered to engage in many of these practices unless they see that top leadership has incorporated them into their regular routines. Remember that bandwidth is about being efficient, effective, and fully alive; organizations that hamper having high bandwidth may be experiencing the opposite in their employees.

A Final Thought

While we mentioned thermometers when talking about a good mindset for the survey, think of your bandwidth score as more like an anemometer reading. With body temperature, high is almost always a reason for concern. But with wind speed, whether or not to be alarmed depends on other factors. Are you hoping to paddle a canoe, where a calm lake is an asset, or take the helm of a sailboat where you need wind in your sails? Is the air temperature 80 degrees or –20 degrees Fahrenheit? Are you sitting in the shade or running in the sun? Whether wind makes life more enjoyable or more difficult depends, doesn't it? Yet knowing the wind speed can make a huge difference in how we dress, what we choose to do, whether we tie on a scarf or wear a hat, and so on.

This book is about using your bandwidth survey results in a similar way and identifying, no matter your circumstances, which habits are helping and which are hindering your ability to fuel, focus, filter information, and stay aligned with your priorities. Here's hoping that like a fresh breeze, these pages will help you clarify what is working and what isn't working in your favor while providing an energizing pathway forward.

Blameless Discernment Moment

1. Which of the six areas are you acing? Think in terms of the role you, others, and circumstances play in your success with this area. How might you use this knowledge to improve bandwidth in another area?
2. Which survey results stood out to you? How did you react to those findings? If you found that you judged yourself, other individuals, groups, or the situation in a way that was harsh or critical, what accounts for your inclination to do so?

Note that we were tempted to add points to the survey for special circumstances such as a new baby in the house, but we decided against it for two reasons. First, since the survey has been statistically validated, adjusting the scores would affect the validity of the results. Second, the score isn't as important as the opportunity to take a true, nonjudgmental appraisal of your current state of brain and bandwidth.

Bandwidth Band Discussion Guide

1. Share a story about a particular bandwidth challenge. Consider specific situations that came to mind as you answered the questions, evidence of how your bandwidth has changed, or an area where you have already taken effective action to improve your brain energy and bandwidth.
2. If you could wave a magic wand, what bandwidth concern would you resolve first and why? What benefits would flow from resolving it?
3. Of the six clusters of survey questions, which area are you least concerned about? Why?
4. Here are the eight items on which participants in our database scored the lowest. What factors in your learning community either increase or decrease your ability to form energizing habits around these areas?
    - I attend to emails at set times rather than constantly.
    - I use power naps to clear my mind.
    - I have regular meditation or yoga or other reflective practices.
    - I avoid multitasking.
    - I set aside uninterruptible blocks of time of at least 60 minutes to work on projects that require deep concentration.
    - When I am driving, I don't text or talk on my phone.
    - I have activities that allow me to relax my mind.
    - I find time to follow my own creative pathways for learning, research, and problem solving.

3

Willpower, Habits, Routines, and Change

Curiosity Creator

Let's say that you struggle to not be the last to leave work at the end of the day. Which of the following strategies would research say is more likely to help you consistently leave on time? Make note of why you chose *A* or *B*.

A. You set a specific goal: *I will leave the building within an hour of the end of the student day.* Since you can see the staff parking lot out the window from your desk, you add that you will pack up if you notice that there are fewer than 10 cars remaining. You also decide that if, on Fridays, you've achieved this goal at least four out of five days, you'll reward yourself with one of your favorite healthy but rather pricy takeaway meals from your favorite deli.

B. You set up an alarm on your phone to play "Heigh Ho, It's Home from Work We Go" (or "It's Been a Hard Day's Night") 50 minutes after the end of the student day. When the song begins, you complete only the next step in whatever you're working on: finishing one email, grading one student's assignment, writing one lesson plan step, and so on. Then you close your laptop, put it in a desk drawer, lock the drawer, put the key in the cupboard farthest from your desk, and walk out.

One of these strategies should work quite well. The other is more likely to lead to less bandwidth, less efficiency, and more frustration. As you read the chapter, see if you can decide which is which—the answer is at the end of this chapter.

Through Chapters 5–10, we'll be helping you decide whether your current bandwidth habits are helpful or not. The chapters end with some specific tips for forming new habits. Here, though, we want to gather two things in one place: the research on what works for changing habits and several universal strategies for doing so.

SMART Goals and Willpower? Sort of . . .

If changing how we usually act was easy, we'd all keep our New Year's resolutions, right? You've probably tried tips for increasing willpower to keep that resolution such as "Write down your goals!" or "Set a SMART (specific, measurable, achievable, relevant, time-bound) goal!" or "Find a buddy for support!" Yet a preponderance of New Year's resolutions fall by the wayside by the third Friday in January, which the fitness community app Strava calls "Quitter's Day."

Trying to persevere via willpower often leaves you short of your goal and feeling depleted. Grit—adding passion to perseverance—often isn't enough. Why? Because you have to change your brain to change a habit or routine. Habits in particular interfere with your brain energy and bandwidth. Habits deliver amazingly enticing rewards to your brain, such as the dopamine we mentioned in Chapter 1. What's more, in order for new brain pathways to get established, known as neuroplastic change, some sort of tamping down of the usual mind map has to take place.

For example, learning a new language can be accelerated by eliminating as much use of the native language as possible so that the new language can build resilient neuroconnections in the brain. The brain doesn't like competing stimuli. This is why practicing reliance on your sense of touch to get around in a dark room works better than if you merely close your eyes; note how you would immediately switch to your preferred mode of using sight if someone switched on a light. In other words, the behaviors that were present first take precedence; if they are greatly attenuated, then new pathways can develop.

Changing habits is hard even though neuroplasticity is a fact. Before you despair, though, remember that *good* habits are good for us. We need habits and routines for efficiency. When taking appraisal of our habits, it's important to take stock of both our good and maladaptive habits and routines.

Neuroscience tells us that automatic behavior plays a large role in our brain energy and bandwidth behaviors. Physiologically, we form habits so that our brains can be efficient. The brain's prefrontal cortex (PFC) uses an exceptional amount of energy as it decides, plans, suggests flexibility, controls impulsivity, and engages in other higher-level functions. If our only way to think was mindful and deliberate, we would soon exhaust ourselves. Everyday choices would quickly become burdensome in the absence of habitual or automatic behavior. One need only consider the number of decisions and actions we undertake from the moment we get up to when we finally lay our heads down to sleep in order to grasp the benefits of doing certain things out of habit. Sleep, in fact, is deeply affected by our sleep *habits,* something we will explore in Chapter 8.

Thus, habits and routines exist for the sake of efficiency. They have an adaptive quality by way of decreasing demands on the prefrontal cortex, moving control of as many behaviors as possible to the basal ganglia. Habits are slightly different from routines in that habits typically have a trigger. As you take stock of your own habits and routines, watch for triggers. They are often tricky to identify, but identifying them is essential to dismantling a maladaptive habit. Generally speaking, changing routines is easier than changing habits, but both require attention and brain energy. Also note that not all triggers lead to maladaptive habits. Triggers can also contribute to the development of healthy and beneficial habits.

Habits in particular help us adapt to our environment. An excellent example of this is how the digital age has created the perfect storm—via notifications, instant gratification, and more—to form a wide assortment of habits that don't serve us well. We were bombarded by stimuli and rewarded by dopamine without knowing we needed strategies to manage the onslaught. Remember that habits automate thinking with routines that are stored in the basal ganglia. Dopamine, the neurotransmitter of reward and motivation, is abundantly present there, rewarding us for both real and perceived efficiencies. Never underestimate its power. You may have heard of experiments in which rats could push one lever to receive dopamine or another lever to receive food, and they starved themselves because they had such a strong craving for dopamine (Wise, 1996).

Understanding Why Habits Are So Hard to Change

In summary, habits themselves aren't the problem; *maladaptive* habits are. Think about checking email repeatedly rather than a few times per day, picking up your phone for no particular reason, or even feeling incomplete if your digital device isn't nearby. Understanding how habits work (action → dopamine reward → deeper embedding of the habit → repeat) helps us see why they're hard to break. Few people consciously thought about what habits might be helpful as the digital age enveloped us. Thus, our brains adapted in ways that don't necessarily benefit us. Think for a moment: did you consciously decide how carrying around a mobile phone affects communicating with family members, sharing what's going on in your life, getting in your workouts, or biding your time while standing in a line?

Changing Maladaptive Habits

Thus, once you identify which engrained habits to change to increase your bandwidth, establishing those new habits will take time. Given that much of our behavior is habitual and automatic, using the best strategies possible to change maladaptive habits will ensure that you don't use up all of your newly created bandwidth while building new habits. Here is what research has found to support moving from an ineffective habit to one that serves you well.

1. **Make one change at a time** (Baumeister & Tierney, 2011). The very nature of change involves brain energy. If you attempt more than one significant change, your efforts will be diluted enough that you may not feel the bandwidth benefit. For example, if your priority is to build a new habit around leaving school at a reasonable hour, experience some success with that goal before adding another.

2. **Establish a clear goal with a clear statement about why reaching this goal is so important to you** (McGonigal, 2011). "This will be good for me" or "I have to do this" simply isn't motivating enough. Instead, for example, envision your "why" for leaving school on time as having extra energy for quality minutes with your children or involving them in meal preparation. Or perhaps leaving on time allows for yoga or a walk while it is still daylight.

3. **Develop a positive attitude** (Judah, Gardner, & Aunger, 2013). Concentrating on the gains rather than the pains is essential. For instance, define why being home on time is important to you. Your gain may be that leaving school on time allows for needed self-care.

4. **Define how you will "swap" one behavior for another** (Juszczyk & Gillison, 2018). Defining a new doable *and* desirable behavior makes it easier to leave behind a maladaptive habit. For example, instead of making sure all emails are answered before you leave school, frame leaving some for the next day as swapping that email routine for a new routine of lengthier and calmer evenings with family or friends. Other examples of swaps include "Instead of binge-watching shows on Sundays, I'm going to set up Zoom visits with friends too far away to see in person" or "I'll turn off all screens an hour before bed and journal." Get as specific as possible. Identify a benefit from this new behavior, or it will have little allure in the face of a well-established habit.

5. **Add an element of fun or engagement** (Kaushal & Rhodes, 2015). Yes, changing habits should be fun, spark a bit of motivating competitiveness, or come with a promise of built-in time doing something you love or some other bonus.

6. **Plan for consistent, supported practice for an average of six weeks** (Wiedemann et al., 2014). If you work with a coach, attend classes or group support meetings, or join with a friend, you are more likely to make and sustain new habits. You're probably not the only educator who needs to develop new habits around leaving work earlier! And while you're at it, add an element of fun to supporting each other, such as singing a song on your way out the door.

7. **Choose simple strategies that lead to new habits** (Kliemann et. al., 2017). You'll see a few simple strategies applied in different ways in the next few pages, such as Cognitive Steps, timers, and the right rewards. For example, if you typically leave school late and come home stressed, you may have started this habit during a particularly busy time. Start to challenge the idea that you can't leave by a reasonable hour by setting a timer, so you're leaving just a bit earlier each week until you reach your goal.

Incorporating these seven elements into your habit-busting plans lets your willpower stretch much further and sets you up for success. But for many habits, you'll also need richer strategies. You'll find specific tips in Chapters 5–10 for changing specific habits, but here are some universal, research-based strategies that put these seven habit-busting research findings into action.

Key Strategies for Developing Good Bandwidth Habits

Name the Gain

Don't just set a goal; articulate with crystal clarity *why* that goal is so important. Why not just state a goal? Why go the extra step of naming why that goal is so important?

Back in 1863, Fyodor Dostoyevsky penned, "Try to pose for yourself this task: not to think of a polar bear, and you will see that the cursed thing will come to mind every minute." He was right. Resisting thoughts takes brain energy. Psychologists now call it ironic process theory (Wegner, 1989). Monitoring our success in *not* thinking about something increases cognitive load, resulting in thinking about it more unless we consciously choose to redirect those thoughts to something else.

If you try to lean away from something, you start reinforcing the wiring that helped form the habit in the first place. Resistance ("I *won't* eat that cookie) still sends energy down that habit's brain pathway. You want to shift to thinking of something else—what you're switching *to*—to create a new pathway. Naming what you'll gain—why you've chosen a new behavior ("I *will* snack on delicious mixed nuts because they fill me up while providing protein and other good things")—changes your focus.

If you say, "I don't want to be online in that hour before bed," you're fighting your brain; it can't tell the difference between "I will be online" and "I won't be online." Your brain only registers that it's thinking about being online. But if you instead say, "Turning off screens an hour before bed will create an hour for reading," your brain will start to form wiring that reinforces your choice of reading.

Thus, when you set a goal, be specific about the gain or improvement you are working toward. Here are some examples.

I want to have the energy at the end of the day to exhibit patience and enthusiasm with my children/spouse, whom I haven't seen all day.

I want to relish any bite or swallow I choose to take, being mindful as I eat.

I want to be in charge of what grabs my attention.

I want a new morning routine that fires me up for my day.

Cognitive Steps

It is a well-known phenomenon that the more effort required to complete a process, the less likely we are to complete it. Thus, we have one-click online shopping. Easy, isn't it? The key to dismantling such automatic behavior is disrupting it with multiple intervening steps. For instance, if you remove your favorite online store apps from your phone and now have to google the site, sign in, *and* remember your password, you just might rethink whether you really need an item.

To help one student who was struggling with his grades make use of cognitive steps, Ann urged him to put his phone in a box, tape it shut, and put it on a high shelf before doing his homework. After a few weeks, he reported that not only had his grades vastly improved, but he actually enjoyed studying. Simply resisting his phone was not enough and was splitting his attention.

Adding multiple cognitive steps made checking social media not worth the effort. Soon, the impulse to check his phone while studying faded away.

Defining Good Enough

The Pareto Principle states that 80 percent of consequences come from 20 percent of causes. This principle has proved true in diverse fields (Newman, 2005). You can use this principle to avoid the bandwidth-draining traps of perfectionism by understanding whether a habit that affects your bandwidth involves the 20 percent of your responsibilities that deserve your absolute best effort.

What are those traps? Perhaps your good intentions get waylaid by an all-or-nothing attitude. For example, believing "if I don't have time to run three miles this afternoon, I should wait until tomorrow" can turn into never finding enough time for a run. Compare that all-or-nothing trap to a school superintendent who, when short on time for a bike ride, heads to a series of hills to get an intense, worthwhile 20-minute workout.

Or perhaps your trap is applying perfectionism to elements that don't deserve it. If you've finished planning a lesson and then spent another half hour searching the internet for a perfect image for a slide or for one more sample problem or something else where the impact isn't worth the effort, you've fallen victim to this trap.

If you've received reinforcement for doing everything perfectly, you may have lost your sense of what is mission critical. Particularly during times of stress, put a mission-critical filter in place to determine what calls for perfection and what can be done adequately. All kinds of questions can help you create this filter, including the following:

- Has it already been done? Can I use what exists?
- Can I borrow part of it or split the effort with someone?
- Should someone else be doing it?
- A week, month, or year from now, will it matter if this is done with perfection?
- Is it vital or nice? Disinfecting surfaces may be vital, but cleaning every speck of marker off whiteboards every day isn't.
- What are the consequences of doing an adequate job versus a perfect job on a particular task?

Building in Slack

In their book *Scarcity: Why Having Too Little Means So Much,* Sendhil Mullainathan and Eldar Shafir (2013) point out the importance of building slack into schedules. They give the example of how a hospital increased the number of surgeries performed by leaving one room unscheduled. You see, emergency surgeries kept bumping out scheduled surgeries. When they created a schedule that accommodated emergencies, they were able to keep up with the scheduled ones.

When you're changing a habit, the principle of slack comes into play. "Give yourself some slack" is actually good advice! How might it apply? Assume, like the hospital, that you might have an urgent matter or two come up. Assume, when you're making a to-do list, that you might not have quite the energy at the end of the week that you're assuming you'll have.

One assumption that can lead to missed deadlines and high stress is that your "personal best" time is your standard time for completing a task. For instance, if you once managed your commute to school in less than 10 minutes, the personal best fallacy leads to the assumption that you can always count on making that drive in less than 10 minutes.

Use Physical Timers

Setting the timer on your phone can keep you in the moment, keep you from multitasking, keep you from worrying, and more (Zahariades, 2015).

Here's a simple example. In Chapter 7 we'll discuss the importance of having a meditation or other mindfulness practice. Let's say you try our strategy of spending two minutes each morning thoroughly enjoying your choice of hot beverage—coffee, tea, matcha, hot chocolate. You take a sip, savor the flavor as the liquid spreads over differing taste buds, enjoy its warmth and smoothness, rub your favorite cup with your fingers—and check the clock to see how long it's been. Then you check it again a few seconds later, interrupting your mindfulness. Or you can set a timer, take a sip and savor, take another sip and savor, close your eyes, and notice the bitter and sweet and tangy and fruity notes, not worrying about monitoring where you are in the two minutes. Can you see how the timer allows you to focus?

Of course, you can't use a timer with the attitude "I have to do this until the timer goes off." Rather, think, "I've given myself this time for this activity, and the timer will let me know when it's time to move on."

Choose the Right Rewards

Remember that our brain chemistry generally rewards us for habits, good or bad. As we're trying to form new habits, different rewards can definitely be motivating. And yet, we often choose rewards poorly, with some (especially food and drink) being brain-draining if not crafted carefully. We get in our own way, overvaluing approaches and outcomes that actually give us less of what we're looking for.

- You tell yourself, "This change of habit is just plain unpleasant. A glass of wine [or favorite comfort food] will help me feel better about it."
- You decide to compete with yourself, setting goals for avoiding social media, and end up discouraged by any failure rather than encouraged by progress.
- You are so afraid of using any treats as rewards that you overlook the benefit of mindfully eating a piece of dark chocolate or using the screen time settings on your phone so that a 15-minute reward of social media doesn't accidentally turn into an hour.
- You want others to acknowledge the benefits of your new habit as motivation, and when they don't, you feel hurt and discouraged.

These are just a few examples. How have rewards backfired on you in the past? Use blameless discernment to decide if you're feeding a different bad habit. If so, try adding an element of fun or competition, or partner with someone.

Remove Triggers and Distractions from Your Environment

Understanding your triggers is an essential part of working with habitual behavior. Identify triggers for your bandwidth-sucking habits. For example, notifications on our electronic devices distract us from whatever we are doing in the present moment. Even if we silence them, they can still divert our attention if we occasionally check the home screen for updates.

Triggers might include a basket of candy that you keep around but indulge in more than you'd like to admit. Or a cluttered desk can trigger the feeling of being overwhelmed. Keeping your phone on your nightstand can set off a cascade of maladaptive habits, including checking it in the middle of the night, lingering over it in the morning, or being disturbed by a light or vibration when you're trying to sleep.

Motivate the Elephant, Shape the Path

Heath and Heath (2010) in their book *Switch: How to Change Things When Change Is Hard* provide a useful framework for planning habit changes. The big challenge in changing a habit is getting the right emotions and motivations involved to ignore the rewards of the old habit long enough to appreciate the rewards of the new. They call this "motivating the elephant." Your rational brain—the rider on the elephant—*knows* what you need to do, but the skinny little reins it has aren't always enough to get the elephant moving in the right direction. The more you shape the path—plan in advance to support yourself in moving in the right direction down the right path—the more likely you'll be successful.

Think of this as a universal strategy that will help you implement many of the suggestions you choose to focus on. Note that you can shape the path via many of the other strategies in this section.

For example, Jane loves crunchy cheese curls. Her brain—the rider—knows that they're crafted to avoid prompting sensory-specific satiating. That means those crunchy little snacks "owe their success to complex formulas that pique the taste buds enough to be alluring but don't have a distinct, overriding single flavor that tells the brain to stop eating" (Moss, 2013). Yup, you can't eat just one. To motivate the elephant, Jane thinks of the *right* times to indulge in this favorite junk food, all centered around not being tempted to eat the whole bag, which just results in feeling awful. So, she shapes the path by (1) never having a bag in the house, knowing that seemingly sound resolutions like "I'm only going to crush them on chili" don't work; (2) declaring when she *can* buy them (to take to a picnic or game day party where she can have her handful and the rest will be gone before she goes back for seconds); and (3) occasionally, if at a sandwich shop with a friend, splitting a snack-sized bag. There. She doesn't have to constantly make decisions about buying cheese curls. And she isn't wasting energy trying *not* to think of buying them.

Similarly, Ann uses elephant/rider/path strategizing to stay on track when engaging with her electronic devices. Her rider knows that apps and websites are designed to keep her engaged by manipulating content that she appears to find interesting. To motivate the elephant, she is clear about what she hopes to gain when she makes a foray into a social media site. To shape the path, she deletes apps and connections that do not serve her stated purpose.

Make a One-Off Choice

A one-off choice is a decision that automates other decisions, decreasing a bit of the load on your PFC and thus leaving bandwidth available for something else. Examples include signing up for a scheduled workout class so that you know exactly when you'll be going rather than buying a pass that means you have to decide when you'll go to 10 random sessions, subscribing to a lecture series with a friend so you have those shared experiences scheduled, or scheduling a weekly time to plan lessons with someone whose skills and work style increase what you can do on your own.

A Final Thought

Look back at the chapter's Curiosity Creator on page 22. Can you see how option B aligns more closely with the research on changing habits? It employs cognitive steps rather than relying, as does option A, on willpower and reward. The song adds a bit of fun. The desired behavior is clear.

Habits and routines are closely linked and also distinctly separate. Habits have triggers, which may be easy to identify or so subtle that we have to look hard to find them. Some of the best examples of habits are the ones that we developed when cell phones and computers exponentially increased connectivity. Our devices didn't come with a user manual that told us how to proactively manage our devices.

Moreover, even though brain energy and bandwidth aren't just about our devices, we developed both device habits and device routines as they became omnipresent in our world. That being said, our hope is that the brain energy and bandwidth assessment will help you examine the many ways your brain is being taxed so that you can develop new habits and routines that will support your effectiveness as an educator and your overall well-being.

How Learning Communities Can Support Habit Changes

Chapters 6–10 each contain five strategies for improving individual bandwidth and five strategies that learning communities might implement to support good bandwidth for everyone. Consider whether your community's norms around the following concepts might interfere.

- How is your mood contagion? See Chapter 5 for the research on how moods spread like viruses through a community
- Is it OK to care for yourself as well as others? See Chapter 4 for information on how this interdependency influences bandwidth.

Blameless Discernment Moment

1. What habits drain you? What habits energize you?
2. Reflect on a habit you have tried to change with less than desirable results. For this habit, figure out one way you could use each of the following strategies:
   - Cognitive steps
   - Name the gain
   - Removing triggers and distractions
   - Rider/elephant/path
   - Clarity on goal and action
   - Swap behaviors
   - Make a one-off choice

Bandwidth Band Discussion Guide

1. As a group, create a Venn diagram showing the differences and similarities between habits and routines. If you want to change a habit or routine, what are some key strategies?
2. Have you changed a habit? If so, what did you change, and what contributed to success?
3. Choose partners to discuss a goal you're contemplating for improving your brain energy and bandwidth. Coach each other to ensure your bandwidth goals include as many of the elements discussed in this chapter as possible.

   - Are you making one change at a time?
   - Is the goal clear, with a clear statement of why reaching this goal is so important to you?

- Do you have a positive "focus on gain, not pain" attitude toward your goal?
- Have you defined a swap of one behavior for another?
- Can you add an element of fun or engagement?
- Do you have a plan for consistent, supported practice for the next six weeks?
- Are you using one of the simple strategies that lead to new habits described in this chapter?

4

My Responsibility and My Community's Responsibility

Curiosity Creator

Three truths and a lie: In the following sets of statements, three are true. Can you pick out the lie?[2]

Set 1

    A. If you don't believe stress can kill you, it won't kill you.

    B. Football teams who go for the 4th down, rather than punting to put the other team in a worse field position, are more likely to win games.

    C. People in India are far more likely to believe that life is short and hard than people who live in North America.

    D. Only about 20 percent of people who experience truly terrifying events develop post-traumatic stress syndrome.

Set 2

    A. Giving other people your time and attention will only make your schedule busier with negligible benefits.

    B. Attending to someone else's needs has been linked to decreased stress levels.

    C. If the stress of caregiving is left unchecked, it can take a toll on your health, relationships, and state of mind.

    D. Tending to others' needs can trigger a "virtuous circle" in which relationships improve, causing us to feel better about ourselves, which leads to more improved relationships.

Apeirogon Thinking

Apeirogons (pronounced a-paragons) are polygons with countably infinite sides. Unlike a cube or even a dodecahedron (12 sides), it's tough to note the exact number of its myriad surfaces.

Likewise, your bandwidth is the result of many, many, many factors. Apeirogon thinking keeps you from misconstruing the source of bandwidth shortages. Here's a partial list of the factors that affect your bandwidth. What might you add?

- Mix of students this year
- Concerns for welfare of students
- Well-being of family members
- Curriculum changes
- Staff changes
- Weather
- Your health
- The political climate
- Relicensing requirements
- Availability of resources
- Parent-teacher-school relationships

We could go on. And that's in a normal year.

Why a fancy term like *apeirogon thinking*? We want to emphasize the importance of reflecting on exactly why your bandwidth is where it is. Look back at the Blameless Discernment exercise in Chapter 1. You may find yourself blaming yourself, others, or circumstances for your decreased bandwidth in this area.

This is my fault. I've tried to fix it before. I'm stuck with it.

This is the fault of [someone else]. There's nothing I can do about it.

This is just temporary. If I get through ___, my score will go up.

While there might be a bit of truth in any of the above, if you define a problem incorrectly, you can't find good solutions. Bandwidth hardly ever results from a single factor. Most of the questions in the survey involve multiple factors. This chapter is about exploring the relationship between individual responsibility and organizational responsibility—with blameless discernment—so that everyone is focused on a holistic way to improve each person's bandwidth. You can't do it alone *and* others can't do it for you.

- Some things are our responsibility. We need to own up to decisions we are making that aren't in our own best interests!
- Our bandwidth is affected by the norms and rules of our organization. Leaders are responsible for creating an environment where everyone is energized, effective, efficient, and engaged.

You *and* Your Learning Community

Figure 4.1 expresses the relationship between your responsibilities and those of your learning community. These aren't polar opposites. Instead, they are intertwined. The goal isn't ensuring a 50:50 balance for responsibility but developing awareness of the facets of each "side" that will go a long way toward getting the best possible long-term outcomes.

Let's look at three related interdependencies to see more of the facets comprising your bandwidth, allowing for apeirogon thinking with blameless discernment.

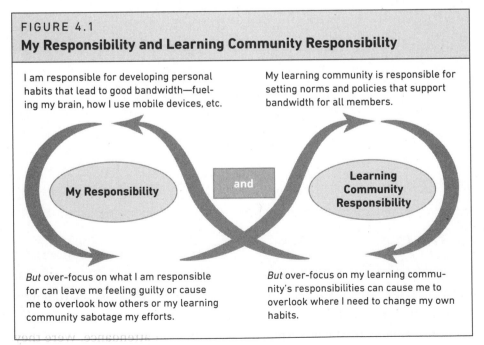

FIGURE 4.1
My Responsibility and Learning Community Responsibility

I am responsible for developing personal habits that lead to good bandwidth—fueling my brain, how I use mobile devices, etc.

My learning community is responsible for setting norms and policies that support bandwidth for all members.

My Responsibility   and   **Learning Community Responsibility**

But over-focus on what I am responsible for can leave me feeling guilty or cause me to overlook how others or my learning community sabotage my efforts.

But over-focus on my learning community's responsibilities can cause me to overlook where I need to change my own habits.

Source: Adapted from Johnson (2020).

Workplace Norms/Expectations *and* Personal Work Habits

The tech firm SAS Institute in North Carolina pushes its employees to strive for a 35-hour work week. They challenge each employee to accomplish as much as they can in that time while taking lunch breaks to ensure they've refreshed themselves physically, socially, and mentally for each afternoon.

What is the norm in your professional community? Do people see putting in long hours as a badge of honor or as a signal that something isn't working? Are meetings a great use of everyone's time, or does time go to agenda items that could be addressed in a memo? Does teacher collaboration save time overall, or is collaboration seen as just "one more thing"?

Yes, children's futures are at stake in our schools. Resources will never be as abundant as in a tech company. SAS is an extreme example. However, workplace norms matter. In fact, they can keep even the most efficient among us from leaving on time, fearing reprimands. To unearth such norms, the Bandwidth survey asks specific questions around organizational support for bandwidth.

- Are you discouraged from checking emails after hours?
- Does leadership seem to respect the boundaries between work and personal life?
- Are meetings a good use of time?
- Does your schedule allow for focused, productive time?

Whatever the norms or policies, though, your personal habits can improve or decrease your bandwidth. As one leader put it, "They are not *asked* to put in 70-hour weeks. Some are choosing to do things, including unimportant things, in ways that aren't efficient or effective." Before you say, "But I can't change that 7 a.m. meeting they expect me to be at," or, "But those papers have to be graded," or anything else that puts the blame back on your learning community, look back at Figure 4.1. We are talking about an interdependency, not you or the leadership being all right or all wrong!

Here's an example of a needed policy that also increased work. Natalie is a high school teacher. Her school adopted a hybrid model for instruction during the COVID-19 pandemic, with some students participating remotely and others in her classroom each day. Understandably, her school's administrators implemented new systems to track student attendance. Were they online when they were supposed to be? Were they participating? What was Natalie doing to improve attendance?

The data was important but laborious to report. In fact, Natalie found that her prep times were consumed by tracking attendance. She seldom had 30–40 minutes to focus on creating lessons that would engage students so that they would *want* to log in for class. You'll learn in Chapter 7 how crucial to efficiency these longer blocks of time for planning really are.

Natalie could

- Only blame herself: "I should be able to do this. I'm terrible at details. So many errors!"
- Only blame others: "Are those administrators crazy? Why can't they just let us teach?"
- Only blame circumstances: "Stupid COVID. Why bother mastering any of this? Things will go back to normal. Meanwhile, they're wasting my time!"

It is so much healthier to identify the nuances of responsibility and brainstorm the steps you might take for optimal methods to increase student attendance. Figure 4.2 shows what Natalie came up with.

Again, blameless discernment is required to ensure you're identifying what you *can* do rather than concentrating on what's being *done* to you.

FIGURE 4.2
My Goal: Planning Time and Tracking Attendance

To gain focused planning time, I might	We might ask administrators to
• Check how other teachers are handling the tracking. Any tricks?	• Reconsider whether all data is essential.
• Think "good enough" on lessons by zeroing in on a few key engaging teaching strategies rather than constantly trying to be original.	• Review data on how much time the tracking consumes.
• Use my Twitter community to see who might swap lessons with me.	• Investigate how to use Zoom reports to automatically track students.
	• Rethink teacher schedules. How can we creatively find more planning time?

Scheduled Time and Personal Time Management

"I have all the time I need to prepare lessons, build relationships with students, provide meaningful feedback, connect with the adults in my students' lives, volunteer for schoolwide initiatives . . . ," said no teacher ever.

We all have the same amount of time. Twenty-four hours in a day. Five workdays in a week. That said, there are huge variations in demands on our time, how we handle time, and how others cut in on our time.

As we dig into the six key areas that contribute to brain energy and bandwidth in the next six chapters, you'll see how making the most of the time we have involves how we leverage our own time and how our professional learning community organizes schedules and respects boundaries. Consider these two questions from the survey:

- I have enough control over my work calendar that I can schedule my days in ways that allow me to be proactive rather than reactive.
- I have time and energy for curiosity at work—pursuing new ideas, problems I'd like to solve, or experiments with creativity.

Can you see the interdependency in each question between how you handle time and how your learning community schedules your time? We've seen schools with such tight schedules that collaborative time seems more like punishment than the gift it should be. This happens when teachers have so little individual prep time that it bleeds over into their personal lives. And we've seen atmospheres where there's barely enough time to master school-driven strategies and initiatives, let alone pursue potential growth in areas of interest to individual teachers.

Yet certain strategies lead to more effective use of the time you have, such as limiting distractions and avoiding multitasking. Again, we need to employ blameless discernment to correctly identify the role we play and the constraints on success put in place by our workplaces to handle time as well as we can.

Outcomes and Relationships

You've probably faced a dilemma like this more than once. There's a baby shower for a colleague, or the all-staff meeting agenda shows "Coffee and Catch-Up" for the first 20 minutes, and your first thought is "I have more important ways to spend my time."

Or you're the administrator. You believe the research that building relationship builds trust, yet there is so much to *do*. So you cut out the "fluff," justifying that collective efficacy comes from making progress toward goals, not just from touchy-feely stuff.

The truth is that improving outcomes and building relationships are interdependent (see Figure 4.3).

It is even more crucial to remember that outcomes and relationships are interdependent when we consider the impact of stress. As stated in Chapter 1, teaching is widely considered one of the most stressful of all professions. The connections between building relationships and showing hardiness in times of stress rest on two important bodies of research.

First, we are hardwired to pay attention to relationships, social status, feelings of inclusion and exclusion, and whether norms and conditions are fair. Maslow's hierarchy of needs proposed that our physiological needs for food, clothing, and shelter are foundational because without them, we fail to thrive. After that came our needs for safety, love, self-esteem, and self-actualization.

Matthew Lieberman (2013) proposes an alternative model: the foundation is our social, not physical, needs. In the absence of human bonding,

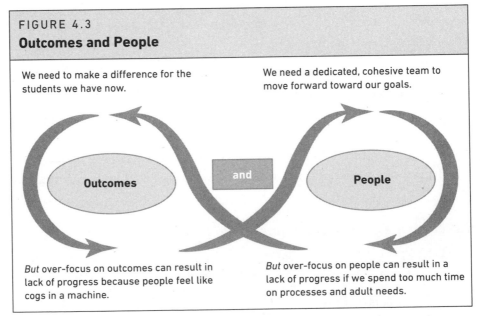

FIGURE 4.3
Outcomes and People

We need to make a difference for the students we have now.

We need a dedicated, cohesive team to move forward toward our goals.

Outcomes   and   **People**

But over-focus on outcomes can result in lack of progress because people feel like cogs in a machine.

But over-focus on people can result in a lack of progress if we spend too much time on processes and adult needs.

Source: Adapted from Kise (2019), p. 147.

which releases a cascade of neurochemicals to support human relationships, we do not survive infancy. Consider the vulnerability of infants. They rely first on the human bond so that their needs are met. Without the neurochemistry to drive this relationship, they would not get the care they needed to survive, let alone thrive. Think of stories you've heard of orphanages where infant physical needs were met, yet, with the relational neglect that flowed from limited staffing, many infants failed to thrive (Hughes, 2013).

The need for relationships is baked into our DNA. It is our first need when we come into the world, and it allowed our ancestors to band together to survive the threats of powerful predators and hostile environments. Glenn Geher and Nicole Wedberg (2020) refer to our need for relationships as a "human universal." Human universals are, essentially, qualities that, due to our shared evolutionary history, characterize humans across the globe.

Second, relationships help us handle stress, especially those relationships where people share the same stress factors. You may have heard oxytocin referred to as the "cuddle" hormone; the emotions of loving and feeling loved cause its release into our bloodstream.

Oxytocin, though, is a stress hormone. The pituitary gland pumps it out, along with adrenaline, when stress levels rise. Stanford professor Kelly McGonigal (2013) explains the healing chain reaction that results *if* you engage in the actions that oxytocin encourages:

- Oxytocin primes you to strengthen relationships, enhances empathy, and makes you more willing to care for those you care about.
- It nudges you to tell others how you feel rather than bottling up those feelings. Your brain wants you to be surrounded by people who care about you, and it urges you to care for those who care about you.
- With its natural anti-inflammatory properties, oxytocin acts on your body, too, protecting your heart from the effects of stress. Through special receptors on the heart, it actually helps heart cells regenerate and heal from stress-related damage.
- Finally, those who act on the impulses oxytocin creates show no stress-related risk of dying. Caring creates resilience. This is *not* true of those who wall up and only care for themselves; their bodies show the negative effects of stress.

"How you think and how you act can transform your experience of stress," says McGonigal (2013). She calls this a "biology of courage" that creates resilience.

The trick to this biology is, of course, to have these relationships in place. And in most cases, your relationships outside the workplace aren't enough. For one thing, professional learning communities are an all-for-one, one-for-all ecosystem. If some people aren't taken care of during stressful times, their stress drags down outcomes for everyone. Further, bringing home workplace stress places strain on personal relationships.

Thus, building relationships is an integral part of a learning community's goal of success for all students. Figure 4.4 provides a framework for considering how to balance this in a learning community.

Do you spend enough time building relationships at work so that you can find support during stressful times *and* engage in time-saving and results-producing collaboration? Does leadership acknowledge the need for such relationships, making space for conversations, experiences, and tasks that nurture them?

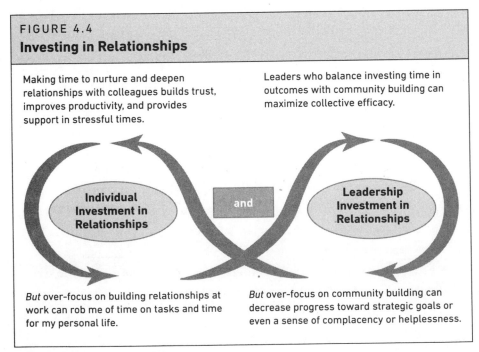

FIGURE 4.4
Investing in Relationships

Making time to nurture and deepen relationships with colleagues builds trust, improves productivity, and provides support in stressful times.

Leaders who balance investing time in outcomes with community building can maximize collective efficacy.

Individual Investment in Relationships

and

Leadership Investment in Relationships

But over-focus on building relationships at work can rob me of time on tasks and time for my personal life.

But over-focus on community building can decrease progress toward strategic goals or even a sense of complacency or helplessness.

Source: Adapted from Johnson (2020).

Caring for Self and Caring for Others

One of the toughest dilemmas for educators is balancing the amount of time we need to devote to self-care with the very real needs of others. Ideally, our lives as educators would be in balance, as in Figure 4.5.

As mentioned in Chapter 1, though, in caring professions such as education and medicine and social work, it may be the norm to get out of balance by devoting too much time to caring for others. Eventually, if we aren't paying enough attention to our own needs, we decrease our capacity to meet the needs of others. And we know that if leaders don't model care of self, those they lead won't feel empowered to care for themselves.

When Jane first introduced this form of both/and thinking to groups of educators, she had them work with the both/and of caring for self and others. Teachers were quick to point out the benefits of caring for others and reported feeling rather selfish as they listed the benefits of caring for themselves. However, when asked "What happens when teachers over-focus on caring for others and neglect their own needs?" the discussion went rather dark rather fast. They noted the high rate of teacher burnout, mentioned

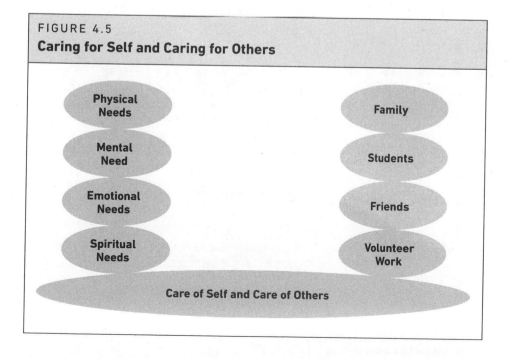

FIGURE 4.5
Caring for Self and Caring for Others

Physical Needs

Mental Need

Emotional Needs

Spiritual Needs

Family

Students

Friends

Volunteer Work

Care of Self and Care of Others

the statistics on teachers and breast cancer (67 percent higher incidence in California than other women; Bernstein et al., 2002), and discussed overall anxiety that whatever they accomplish for students won't be enough. They needed permission to care for themselves in the ways that would allow them to have the energy their students need and be in education for the long haul.

When you look at Figure 4.6, where are you on the loop? Experiencing the interdependent upsides? One of the downsides? Use blameless discernment to consider your role and the norms of your learning community to understand why you are currently experiencing this position.

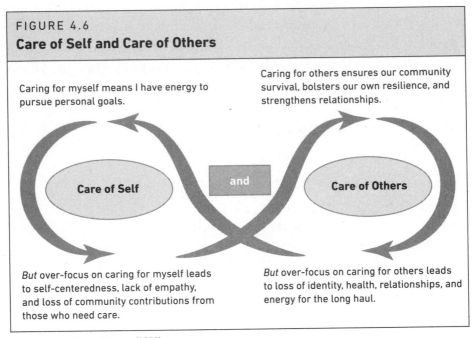

FIGURE 4.6
Care of Self and Care of Others

Caring for myself means I have energy to pursue personal goals.

Caring for others ensures our community survival, bolsters our own resilience, and strengthens relationships.

Care of Self

and

Care of Others

But over-focus on caring for myself leads to self-centeredness, lack of empathy, and loss of community contributions from those who need care.

But over-focus on caring for others leads to loss of identity, health, relationships, and energy for the long haul.

Source: Adapted from Johnson (2020).

Creating a Bandwidth Culture

We've identified four key areas where both/and thinking about individual and community responsibility can create more bandwidth for everyone:

- Workplace norms/expectations and personal work habits
- Scheduled time and personal time management
- Outcomes and relationships
- Care of self and care of others

As you've seen, the key to bandwidth for everyone is blameless discernment around how *you* can improve your own bandwidth and how *leaders* can shift norms and policies that might improve everyone's energy, effectiveness, and engagement. Chapters 5–10 are about ways to improve your own bandwidth. Now let's look at two key organizational imperatives: leadership styles and data-informed bandwidth discussions.

Leaders: Is Your Style Messing Up Effectiveness and Engagement?

Whether you are a district leader, building leader, teacher leader, outside consultant, parent leader, or someone else in a position of influence, your work style has an effect on others. Here are some key areas for self-reflection. We encourage you to carve out time to ponder each one of these *and* pass your conclusions by someone who knows you well and is affected by your style.

1. *How well do you handle stress?* Stress management is a component of emotional intelligence in many common assessments. However, with the tool we use, the EQi-2.0 from Multi Health Systems, too much of any component can derail leaders as easily as too little can. What's the downside of excellent stress management? Inadvertently, your desire to show strength and competence in the face of a storm might make others wonder why they can't keep up! Take a moment to consider your most effective stress management strategies. Consider what it looks like when you overuse them. Do you need to adjust to be a more realistic and helpful role model for others?

2. *How good is your grasp of reality?* Collective teacher efficacy, defined as an atmosphere where teachers believe that they have the capacity to reach the goals set out for them and that their hard work will have the desired results (Sun & Leithwood, 2015), has an effect size on student learning of 1.57, according to John Hattie (Corwin Visible Learning, n.d.). That means when collective efficacy is present, students may make nearly four times the progress expected in a year.

   Sometimes in fear of setting goals that aren't big enough, we fall into what Jane calls the "Man on the Moon Trap." Yes, the country rose to John F. Kennedy's challenge of putting a man on the moon before the end of the 1960s, but the estimated cost in today's dollars was over $150 billion. For a school, costs include time, monetary resources, professional development resources, competing initiatives, outside pressures such as changing laws or civil unrest, and more.

As you set the vision, are your goals too big, too small, or just right? Do they create the kind of collective efficacy that leads to staff energy? Or do they lead to discouragement?

3. *Are you modeling bandwidth-enhancing habits and promoting self-care?* We outlined the research around the crucial fact that if leaders don't model self-care, no one else in the organization feels empowered to do so. The same goes for bandwidth-improving habits such as checking emails at set times during the day and engaging in a mindfulness practice (see Chapter 7).

4. *How else might your personal style affect the bandwidth of those you lead?* Consider asking a trusted colleague to look at the bandwidth questions, especially the outcomes questions, and comment anywhere your habits or mode of operation positively or negatively affect others.

Your reflections might become your personal to-do list for improving everyone's bandwidth. However, remember as we stated in Chapter 3, don't try to change everything at once! Sometimes you can identify a quick change to policy that will result in more bandwidth for everyone. One example is to stop sending any emails after the end of the school day so that no one feels pressured to answer them (and don't schedule them all for 7 a.m. the next morning so that teachers are overwhelmed before they get their coats off).

Have a Data-Informed Discussion

Chapter 11 provides a case study on how you can use the survey data to home in on priorities in your learning community. Where is bandwidth lowest? How did we get to where we are? What can we learn from what is working or not working?

Then, imagine a session where everyone takes an attitude of blameless discernment. We'll save the details for Chapter 11, but such a session would include both individual and community responsibility:

- A report from leadership that includes what the community is doing well as well as areas of concern.
- Communication of any immediate steps that leaders have recognized they can take to help everyone's bandwidth level improve.
- Time for group brainstorming of ways to change norms and expectations to better leverage outcomes and people.
- Individual commitment to one bandwidth-improving habit they plan to change.

Final Thoughts

You are and aren't responsible for your current bandwidth score. Apeirogon thinking is a healthy way to blamelessly discern your own responsibility for reclaiming your energy, passion, and time *as well as* identify where learning community norms get in everyone's way.

Ponder how well you are balancing these interdependencies:

- Workplace norms and your work habits
- Scheduled time and personal time management
- Outcomes and relationships
- Caring for self and caring for others.

There is no once-and-for-all strategy for balancing any of these interdependencies. Circumstances change. Staff changes. Priorities change. Outside forces change—if anything, the COVID-19 pandemic taught us to not get complacent about how we approach anything!

Hopefully, this chapter helps guide your thinking about how you can best improve bandwidth on your own and where you might advocate for learning community norms to help everyone reclaim their energy, passion, and time.

Blameless Discernment Moment

1. Sometimes your environment makes it easier to strive toward enhanced outcomes. Sometimes people, policies, and circumstances seem to get in the way. Like a ship on a stormy sea, the challenges might be great, but the consequences of not making a few adjustments to stay on course might be even greater. Take a moment to discern

what your sea might look like in your current situation and what you might do to navigate it.

2. Consider Figure 4.6. Are you contented with how you are juggling the many facets of each of these? Here are some areas for reflection:
   - Do I have relationships in place that I can turn to for support?
   - Am I appropriately sharing my load at work and in my personal life, or do I try to do it all?
   - How well am I tending to my physical, spiritual, emotional, and social needs?
   - In what ways do I comfortably care for others?
   - What boundaries have I set to ensure I don't do for others what they should do for themselves?

Bandwidth Band Discussion Guide

1. Watch the TED Talk "How to Make Stress Your Friend" (McGonigal, 2013) on YouTube. Discuss how you might change your approach to stress.
2. Individually complete the following chart. Then compare answers. Which quadrant was hardest for each of you to complete? What insights about your own mindset did you gain from hearing others' responses?

What positive results flow from focusing on self-care?	What positive results flow from focusing on caring for others?
1. 2. 3.	1. 2. 3.
What problems might arise if you over-focus on self-care and neglect caring for others?	What problems might arise if you over-focus on caring for others and neglect self-care?
1. 2. 3.	1. 2. 3.

3. Identify one change you'd like to see in your learning community as well as a potential action step, and share it with the group.

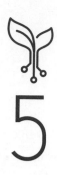

5

Balancing Priorities to Maximize Hardiness

From the Bandwidth Survey

_____ I feel rested when I get up in the morning.

_____ I have activities that allow me to relax my mind such as reading, listening to music, TV, or web surfing.

_____ I make sure I take time for rest when I am ill.

_____ After work, I still have plenty of patience for the most important people in my life.

_____ I feel satisfied with the amount of time I spend with family and friends.

_____ At important family and personal events or outings, I can keep my mind in the moment and let work issues go.

_____ I take advantage of opportunities to maintain relationships with my coworkers.

Curiosity Creator

Before you read this chapter, reflect on the following questions:

1. What strategies do I use to help protect my personal life from my work life?
2. What colleagues can I lean on for empathy, perspective, and advice?
3. When did I last spend quality time with a friend? What did we do?
4. What do I do when I need to turn off my brain and relax?
5. How do I know when I am too sick to go to work?

Powerful Priorities

Do you feel in control of your life, or does your life feel out of control? We can't control what our day will bring, much like we can't control whether the ocean will be calm or turbulent. However, we can develop our ability to surf the prevailing conditions on any given day. One "surfing" strategy is to develop a crystal clear focus on your true priorities. When Greg McKeown (2014) wrote, "While other people are complaining (read: bragging) about how busy they are, you will just be smiling sympathetically, unable to relate. While other people are living a life of stress and chaos, you will be living a life of impact and fulfillment" (p. 232), he was referring to people who have taken the time to narrow down all the possibilities and responsibilities that are most essential to them.

"But everything on my list is essential!" you might be thinking. You may even be trying several different time-saving strategies or life hacks to make it all work. Perhaps you scored well on this section of the bandwidth survey, indicating that you indeed are juggling the complex demands of life well. However, if your score is lower than you'd like, how much stress are you experiencing? That stress produces cortisol. While cortisol improves our thought processes and reflexes in stressful situations, the long-term impact is different. Unmitigated chronic stress, with the accompanying constant exposure to cortisol and other factors, decreases our ability to learn (Medina, 2014) and to handle emotions (Jung et al., 2019). It also leads to impaired cognitive ability that is associated with developing dementia (de Souza-Talarico et al., 2011).

Ineffective methods of managing stress deplete that precious bucket of bandwidth you need to regulate emotions, apply willpower, persevere, and more. Trying to do everything decreases the chances that you'll be able to do anything! This chapter is about naming your essential priorities so that you are at peace with how you are handling work and life.

Look at the interdependent relationship between work life and personal life in Figure 5.1. This is another system, like the ones we explored in Chapter 4, that deserve both/and thinking to be applied to your life rather than only either/or.

The left side of Figure 5.1 captures some of the motivations for educators and our passion for making a difference as we earn a living. The questions in this section of the bandwidth survey capture the value of our personal life.

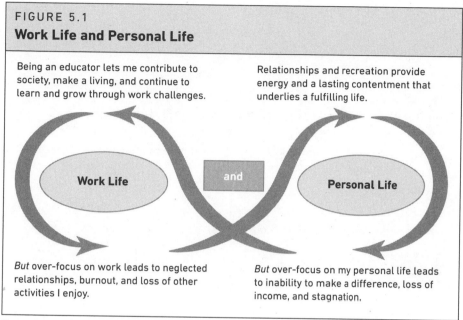

FIGURE 5.1
Work Life and Personal Life

Being an educator lets me contribute to society, make a living, and continue to learn and grow through work challenges.

Relationships and recreation provide energy and a lasting contentment that underlies a fulfilling life.

Work Life   and   Personal Life

But over-focus on work leads to neglected relationships, burnout, and loss of other activities I enjoy.

But over-focus on my personal life leads to inability to make a difference, loss of income, and stagnation.

Source: Adapted from Johnson (2020).

Why aren't there questions for the work side? That side is already honored in education. After all, busy-ness gets the most kudos in our society!

We assume that if you're reading this book, you're already dedicated to your career. You may be surprised that some of the strategies for becoming more effective in your work actually start with nurturing your personal life. However, you saw in Chapter 1 the high levels of stress and burnout in the profession. Yes, you know you need a personal life, but without reflection on priorities, the right pieces might not get the right attention. The questions related to these priorities in the survey highlight the components of the other side (relationships and recreation) that fuel your ability to help students over the long haul. In other words, paying attention to relationships, recreation, *and* work is a key factor in staying energized for the journey.

Work/Life Balance Is a Journey, Not a Destination

Often, people talk about "finding the right balance between work and personal life." And that makes it sound like it's one and done, like getting the right number of rocks on each side of a balancing scale. However, look at Figure 5.2. How have the "rocks" changed in your life over the course of a week, month, year, or season of life? We're constantly readjusting!

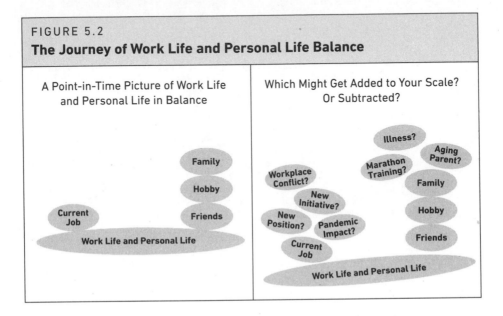

FIGURE 5.2
The Journey of Work Life and Personal Life Balance

So saying "If only I could find the right balance, I could reduce my stress" isn't a productive approach.

Instead, try "If I can identify what is important in each area of life and find a way to navigate this ongoing journey, I can be content." For example, one school district administrator knew that family came first and changed a simple habit, telling us, "After work, I have the most patience for the most important people in my life when I make time to decompress by sitting still and allowing peace to penetrate me. If I skip this step, I am not the same person."

A stress-free life isn't the goal, nor is it meaningful. In fact, the only real way to avoid stress is to avoid goals and avoid relationships. And that's not much of a life. So how do we handle an inherently stressful career *and* have a life?

The key is how you view stress. The most useful framework we've found for approaching stress is a concept called hardiness: the ability to grow from stress.

Hardiness: The "Right" View on Stress

Defined by Salvatore Maddi (2005), research has shown that being hardy is in some ways the secret sauce of stress management (Kovács & Borcsa, 2017), improving both our psychological and physical stamina. And hardiness has a lot to do with managing your priorities. So what is it? The following questions capture the components of hardiness. Reflect on whether you foster this quality or unwittingly leak brain energy and bandwidth by bypassing these important needs.

1. Do you see stress as a normal aspect of life and an opportunity to grow?

In the 1970s, as the compounding effects of Watergate, the oil crisis, inflation, the early signs of climate change, and more began to wear on people's optimism, M. Scott Peck's *The Road Less Traveled* (1978) sent shock waves through society with its message about how facing problems often makes us feel frustrated, lonely, guilty, anxious, and more.

> These are uncomfortable feelings, often very uncomfortable, often as painful as any kind of physical pain, sometimes equaling the very worst kind of physical pain . . . and since life poses an endless series of problems, life is always difficult and is full of pain as well as joy. (p. 16)

Somehow this message, from a book that spent the equivalent of 13 years on the *New York Times* bestseller list, has gotten lost. Think of the discussions about whether 2020, with the combined storm of pandemic, political unrest, social justice crises, and climate-related disasters, was the worst year ever. Elders who had lived through 2001, 1973, 1968, 1963, 1942, 1929, 1918, and so on might have other opinions. Or they might agree with Peck that life is difficult; in every year, people in some circumstances experience the worst year of all times. The question is how do we persevere, survive, and even continue to thrive in inevitable turbulent times, whether the circumstances are personal, national, or global?

Part of the modern struggle is the attention to happiness as an inalienable right. "Inalienable" simply means that a right doesn't derive from a deity or from others or from law; it is a natural right. All humans have the right to pursue happiness. However, we've become confused about what leads to happiness.

In *The Hacking of the American Mind,* Robert Lustig (2017) points out that we're confused by the instant dopamine-driven feelings of happiness and pleasure. These come from the sensation connected with "I want more!" we experience in

- Mindlessly eating simple carbs and sugar.
- Social media "likes."
- Drug highs.

This contrasts with the serotonin-driven feelings of contentment and well-being—the internal sensation connected with "this is good and I have enough." Confuse the importance of the two, and misery follows.

Hardy people concentrate on contentment, knowing that the pursuit of happiness as a driving purpose won't be as fulfilling as a life of contentment and pursuit of meaning. An instructional coach told us that the pandemic helped her "set more realistic goals and feel fulfilled and satisfied when things are not Great or the Best, but simply better than yesterday." Being content with those realistic goals was the key.

2. During difficult times, do you stay engaged with life or move to isolation?

Do you stay connected with others during stress, collaborating with colleagues and reaching out to friends and family?

Perhaps reflecting on the COVID-19 pandemic is the perfect way to test your natural reaction to stress. On the work side, did you stay in contact with other educators, share ideas, and engage in productive ways of supporting each other? Or did you isolate yourself other than for required meetings?

On the personal side, did you find ways to meaningfully connect with family and friends that you couldn't see in person when public spaces were closed and gatherings were restricted?

As we've discussed, our need to connect with others is baked into our ancestral DNA. Those early humans would not have survived if they had not banded together; modern humans still have those social needs.

3. When teaching brings on stress, do you continue to make choices to change the situation or change how it is affecting you?

Do you look for ways to take action rather than turning hostile or self-defensive?

In his book *Essentialism,* Greg McKeown (2014) points out how we often view our choices as finite things when really there is a distinction between the options we are presented with and the actions we decide to take.

> For too long, we have overemphasized the external aspect of choices (our options) and underemphasized our internal ability to choose (our actions). . . . Options (things) can be taken away, while our core ability to choose (free will) cannot be. (p. 35)

This factor is the difference between seeing yourself as a victim and seeing yourself as an agent. Are you using your ability to choose? We want to acknowledge that the source of some stressors, such as systemic racism, go beyond the scope of bandwidth. And yet, think of those who fight these injustices. Can you see evidence of their hardiness?

4. Do you take care of yourself physically, emotionally, and spiritually?

Chapter 8 covers the physical aspects of self-care in-depth, but in terms of bandwidth and hardiness, physical self-care is insufficient. Relationships and recreation are the balancing factors to your work life. They aren't in the category of "nice" but rather are crucial to bandwidth, as you'll discover in the next section.

Hardiness Through Relationships and Recreation

We hope we've made it clear that balancing priorities isn't about fitting in more, perfecting time management skills, getting up earlier, or specific techniques for chore lists. Instead, it is about knowing your true priorities and making choices that keep those things a priority. In other words, you seek a serotonin-driven life instead of only a dopamine-driven life. Four big factors related to bandwidth can guide you in targeting where you might focus:

1. Valuing recreation
2. Focusing on people as well as on tasks
3. Being present wherever you are
4. Choosing your reactions

Let's look at these one by one.

Valuing Recreation

If you haven't noticed, our culture is productivity-minded. Often, we act as if we (and those around us) are machines, working at a steady rate whenever they are on and doing absolutely nothing when they are turned off. Human productivity, though, does not work this way. In fact, productivity *decreases* over time for us; rest is just as essential to work! We'll cover three components of recreation: rest, recreational activities, and doing nothing.

First, let's look at rest. While we will go into sleep more deeply in Chapter 8, consider your attitude toward rest.

Do you take for granted being tired when you wake up? We know that many educators rely on alarm clocks to drag themselves to work by a phenomenally early hour. Crucial to bandwidth is getting the sleep you need.

The adage may be to get eight hours of sleep, but the majority of us need between seven and nine hours. Have you ever experimented to find out your true need? One of the keys to knowing how to feel well-rested is to keep a sleep diary. Observe your sleep habits. Use blameless discernment (don't judge yourself or get frustrated) to notice what helps you get a good night's rest and what stands in the way. How to be well-rested is a bit of a puzzle to be solved!

Do you slow down when you are ill? Perhaps the COVID-19 pandemic helped society change from a nation of martyrs who drag themselves to work no matter what to a national attitude of "Don't go when you're ill. It's about others! Stay home and get back to 100 percent faster!" Hopefully educators also learned how digital platforms can ease the stress of preparing to have a substitute teacher fill in for you. Imagine having some core lessons that can be flexibly inserted into your unit plans available for asynchronous learning. Or perhaps you don't have to imagine, as your learning community has already implemented this practice. Not only is this the end of "free movie" days, but it's the end of an ill and panicked teacher trying to leave a meaningful assignment for an unknown substitute to implement.

Second, let's look at recreation. Recreation seems like a luxury, but recreating yourself to be more creative, more patient, more efficient, and more engaged is essential. Try changing the pronunciation. You are "re-creating" yourself. Hopefully that highlights its importance!

In the book *Rest: Why You Get More Done When You Work Less,* Alex Soujung-Kim Pang (2016) explains how work and rest should be inherently linked.

> When we think of work and rest as opposites, or treat exercise as something that would be good to do when we finally have the time, we risk becoming like the low achievers in [a study]. We shouldn't be surprised that people manage to be physically active and do world-class work. We should recognize that they do world-class work because they are physically active. (p. 196)

He points to countless studies and examples of icons in every field who see their leisure pursuits as essential to their work as time practicing, experimenting, inventing, writing, leading, practicing medicine . . . the principle holds true in every field. Whether you, like Einstein and his violin, recreate your bandwidth through music or through running like prize-winning author Haruki Murakami and many others or through quilting or woodworking or rock climbing or strategy games—or so many other fulfilling pursuits—prioritizing your recreational pursuit is crucial to making a difference in your work life. Pang points out a blind spot in the research on high performance: scientists and researchers have only looked at the forms of work these people engage in.

> This is how we've come to believe that world-class performance comes after 10,000 hours of practice. But that's wrong. It comes after 10,000 hours of deliberate practice, 12,500 hours of deliberate rest, and 30,000 hours of sleep. (p. 74)

Have you found a "deliberate rest" practice? It might be

- Artistic—music, drama, drawing or painting, or a craft.
- Physical—a sport or activity you love and strive to build skills in.
- Mental—playing chess or other games, reading something unrelated to work, or learning a new language.
- Spiritual—meditation or other disciplines.

We'll address in Chapter 8 the question of "How is someone with small children, a health condition that zaps energy, a caregiver for elderly parents, or something else supposed to find time?" For now, ponder the truth that finding time for these seemingly unproductive pursuits makes you more productive!

Third, we need absolute downtime. This is time when you allow yourself to have no goals and no thoughts about solving world hunger. We need to daydream for (1) creativity, (2) to make sense of interactions with other people, and (3) to create our sense of self (Smart, 2013). This means that yes, television is recreational as long as it doesn't spiral into binge-watching that keeps you from your other priorities. Nardi (2011) used EEG technology to examine leisure activities, such as playing games and reading. He found that watching TV evokes the least brain activity of leisure activities (the exceptions being highly emotional or complex content, such as *The Notebook* or *Memento*).

Multiple cognitive scientists have postulated that when your brain appears to have gone offline, it is actually engaged in intuitive thought. In his book *Creativity*, Mihaly Csikszentmihalyi (2009) wrote, "Cognitive theorists believe that ideas, when deprived of conscious direction, follow simple laws of association. Free from rational direction and predictable direction, ideas can combine and pursue each other every which way" (pp. 101–102).

Gallate et al. (2012) found that creative people who take breaks and engage in "nonconscious processing," better known as daydreaming, are more productive and creative than those who eschew such breaks. Incubating ideas is a real thing—and doing so requires true downtime for your brain.

A good example of creative downtime actually happened during a pandemic centuries ago. Isaac Newton, who was described as idle and inattentive by his teachers, discovered the universal law of gravity while being idle at his parents' farm during the Bubonic Plague of 1665.

If you're finding it hard to value resting and recreating, you are not alone. As you go through the ways to improve bandwidth in this area, consider banding with colleagues to hold each other accountable and claim these essential priorities for finding the contentment that leads to true satisfaction with work life and personal life.

Focus on People, Not Just Tasks

The best schools have an atmosphere of trust and collective efficacy. You need to feel part of a family, not just show up and leave. Aristotle asserted long ago in his *Politics,* "Man is by nature a social animal. . . . Anyone who either cannot lead the common life or is so self-sufficient as not to need to, and therefore does not partake of society, is either a beast or a god" (Book 1, Chapter 2).

In *Social: Why Our Brains Are Wired to Connect,* Matthew Leiberman (2013) captures why—whether you're introverted or extraverted—you need colleagues and interaction. Only a very few species have friendships; our human brains evolved in ways that enable these social connections. Relationships are the foundation for motivation in our work. Lieberman suggests that it isn't money; paying for performance turns out to be a poor motivator. Drawing on the motivational business psychology of David Rock, Lieberman presents the SCARF model of motivation—people are intrinsically motivated by five fundamental factors: status, certainty, autonomy, relatedness, and fairness—and three of these five factors (status, relatedness, and fairness) are social in nature.

Most educators have now internalized that teaching shouldn't be a solo profession; one of the factors that has the greatest impact on student learning (Corwin, n.d.) is collective teacher efficacy, defined as an atmosphere where teachers believe that they have the capacity to reach the goals set out for them and that their hard work will have the desired results (Sun and Leithwood, 2015). *Collective* is key. Schools where teachers are working successfully toward these common goals have a deep atmosphere of trust where people can take risks, learn from mistakes, and feel supported as they do so, much like a family. And for that atmosphere to exist, the adults need to know each other and collaborate effectively.

Having good friends has a substantial effect on your quality of life. Nattavudh Powdthavee (2008) used the shadow pricing method to estimate the monetary values of life satisfaction gained by an increase in the frequency of interaction with friends, relatives, and neighbors. Using the British Household Panel Survey, he found that an increase in the level of social involvements is worth up to an extra £85,000 (approximately US$100,000) per year in terms of life satisfaction. Actual changes in income, on the other hand, buy very little increase in the same measure of happiness. Cultivating a support-ive friend at work increases your chances of regularly seeing someone who will contribute to your life in this profound way.

Further, if you're a school leader, know that if you focus on results, you have a 14 percent chance of being seen as a top-tier leader. If you are also able to foster good relationships in your learning community, that chance skyrockets to 72 percent (Zenger & Folkman, 2009). Relationships matter at least as much as achieving results—in fact, it's amazingly difficult to get good results without focusing on people. Getting results and caring for people are interdependent!

Leaders are also responsible for the overall tone of the community. Considering your brain energy and bandwidth, why is it important to strive to keep conversations positive rather than negative? Why would collective negativity drain your brain energy? The phenomenon known as emotional contagion suggests that one person's emotions and related behaviors directly trigger similar emotions and behaviors in other people. Have you ever walked into a room and felt a mood before hearing a single word?

Emotional contagion (Hatfield, Cacioppo, & Rapson, 1993) describes the phenomenon where individuals tend to express and feel emotions that are similar to those around them. When someone tells you with a big smile that she is expecting her son to visit next week, you smile also. In contrast, if a friend tells you his cat died, you feel the weight of it not because you're a cat lover or that you knew the cat, but because your friend is sad. In other words, your friend's emotional state influences your own. Emotional contagion is in fact a form of social influence.

Emotional contagion may occur between two people and in larger groups. Think of collective rage that spreads among a group of workers when they feel they are asked to implement impossible work initiatives. Consider the panic that flowed through teaching communities because of concerns over health and safety during COVID-19. Emotions are, in large part, elicited because people catch each other's emotions: people are sad, elated, fright-ened, or angry because they see others in their immediate surroundings experiencing these emotions. In the case of a pandemic with a high level of uncertainty, it is easy to default to a collective panic rather than a mindset that looks for creative solutions.

According to psychoanalyst Thomas Arizmendi (2011), "What we have learned is that by observing another's actions or even hearing them (audio-visual mirror neurons), the same area of the brain becomes activated that would if we were performing that action ourselves. In other words, the same neurons fire when we perform that action or merely observe it" (p. 408). Current research is studying precisely what goes on in the brain that allows us to catch and feel an emotion from others.

Being Present with Family and Friends

What we're calling rest and recreation, Alex Pang (2016) calls "deep play." Even when the same skills are used—such as nurturing children while teaching or parenting—clear boundaries are crucial. Using the example of a technical sport such as rock climbing, he summarizes with the following:

> You may feel that rock climbing is like science, but you can't work on equations while you're hanging thirty feet off the ground. Unlike efforts to achieve work-life balance that end up smearing the two worlds together and lead to your multitasking your way through children's activities, deep play demands exclusive focus. (p. 219)

Friendships, marriage, parenting, and deep play require deep presence—we can't have half our mind back at school and half in the moment. Why?

First, being present in body but not in spirit often increases our guilt—we're at the soccer game *and* we don't see our child kick a goal, or we have to admit to someone we care about "Sorry, I missed what you were saying; my mind was back in the office." Up goes stress; down goes bandwidth.

Second, those we care about notice. Research on how children try to get the attention of parents who are on their devices, whether for work or to check in on social media, indicates an increase in unpleasant parent-child interactions (Radesky et al., 2016). While technology can provide some flexibility in schedules as well as effectively engage children when parents need to complete tasks, parents report both inner tensions and unpleasant interactions with children who feel—and are justified in feeling—they are competing for their parents' attention.

Rather than this vicious cycle, Natalie, a high school teacher with a toddler, recommends always having a list of activities you can try if something isn't working. Don't attempt to stretch your brain by getting clever in the moment. Be ready! This lets you be more present with your work so that you can be fully present later with your child. At school, Natalie sets clear boundaries around when she is available to answer emails and other questions from her students and coworkers.

Parent-child interactions are often complex; it isn't easy to task-switch between something at work and the needs of a child. Parents report feeling stressed by competing priorities and by not adequately responding to their children. Again, not being fully present decreases efficiency, dampens contentment, and depletes bandwidth. One school principal shared a much-appreciated action step: "Over the Thanksgiving break, our superintendent told us that we were not to email each other or respond to any email. He gave us a specific out-of-office message that we were to all use for the weekend."

Third, if you keep a social commitment but aren't really present as your mind spins on ("I have work to do. How are we going to make that deadline?"), you lose the rejuvenating power of socializing *and* you still have the work to do. It's doubly draining! How can you be present when you really *do* have work to do? Try using your phone timer to cue you that it's time to leave rather than using bandwidth to keep checking. Here's how a timer might shift being present at a picnic. Remember, the relationship between time and productivity isn't linear!

- No timer? You grab your food and sit by the person you most need to connect with, all the time checking your watch to see if it's time to leave. You don't dare join in a game because you might have to leave. You leave early because you aren't having fun anyway and you might as well get a head start on the project that is all-consuming. You didn't recreate at the event. Distracted and feeling rather miserable about not enjoying this infrequent event, you have to stay up late to finish the project.

- Timer? You decide that you can easily spend 90 minutes at the picnic and still finish the project before bedtime. You chat with various friends or relatives, join in the balloon toss, enjoy appetizers with one group, eat a salad while chatting with others, and relax on the lawn with an old friend until the timer goes off. You're fully present at this event to which you gave priority, recreating yourself so you have the capacity to finish the project in record time.

Choosing Reactions

Finally, people who prioritize rest and recreation are more patient, kind, considerate, and empathetic. They handle stress better. They are able to tap their emotional intelligence. Remember, you have one bucket of bandwidth. If your emotional responses in your personal life aren't what you hope for, you've probably drained that bucket at school. Tapping it for complex tasks, for handling student needs, for not eating those stale cookies in the staff lounge—without refueling it through rest and recreation and relationships— means the bandwidth isn't there for regulating emotions.

Although improved self-awareness will help you begin to recapture the capacity for improved reactions to your everyday stressors, the real progress will be made when new habits are formed. Forming new habits does expend brain energy on the front end, but once invested, the benefits are enormous.

A Final Thought

Are you constantly wondering whether you're choosing the right priorities? Consider this thought from Facebook CEO Sheryl Sandberg (2005): "If I had to embrace a definition of success, it would be that success is making the best choices we can . . . and accepting them" (p. 140).

While you may quibble with how she herself has pursued success, her definition can be a useful tool for blameless discernment. If you know your priorities—for work, for relationships, for recreation—and make choices with them in mind, isn't accepting them a healthy mindset?

Blameless Discernment Moment

So many mindsets can get in the way of this kind of contentment with choices. Do any of these traps keep you constantly looking over your shoulder, wondering if you're where you "should" be and doing what you "should" be doing? If so, let them go. Below is a tip for each, all of which you might customize by revisiting the key strategies for changing habits.

- **The perfectionism trap.** Are you always trying to be the perfect parent or caregiver or friend? Or are you trying to be the perfect teacher, grading in exemplary ways rather than incorporating student self-assessment or peer feedback? Or are you trying to be the perfect cook, thinking that homemade has to be all from scratch?
- **The sequentialism trap.** Do you tend to work through your to-do list in order rather than checking off first what bugs you most or what is most important? Instead of a first-on, first-off approach to that list, what if you wrote the items on sticky notes so you can reprioritize?
- **The overcommitment trap.** Do you tend to say yes in the moment, let others volunteer you, or stay involved even after something isn't a passion for you because "someone has to do it," or through other mechanisms end up overcommitted? Learn to say, "I need to check my calendar. I'll let you know later." This pause allows you to consider the fit with your priorities.
- **The presentism trap.** Does short-term thinking, such as "It's faster to do this myself," get in the way of long-term efforts, such as being able to delegate or shift your responsibilities? Understanding the "why" is key to exiting this trap.
- **The guilt trap.** To whom are you comparing yourself that you struggle to be content with your choices? Where do you need a reality check on what is humanly possible? Reconsider the survey questions for balancing priorities. About what area do you feel guilty? What is a small step you can take? Which of the key strategies from Chapter 3 can help you make that change and end the guilt trip/trap?

Five Individual Pathways for Balancing Priorities

1. **Look for synergy.** If you're in a season of life when finding time for recreating is tough, get creative in intentional ways to fulfill two priorities in one activity. For example, Jane found time for piano lessons with the same teacher as her children *and* combined practicing with quality time as they played duets and trios together. Recreation and

relationships can be rolled into one activity. You can spend time with an important person while cooking dinner; just involve a child or friend. Think both/and rather than either/or.

2. **Be present.** Enjoy what you are doing. Where is the awe in what a child can do or in the flavor of what you are eating? As you train yourself to slow down and be present, you will be amazed at what you didn't notice before. When you really begin to see the mosaic of trees in the forest or hear the songbirds of spring, it will be ample reinforcement that being present has a substantial impact on your brain bandwidth.

3. **Make a one-off choice.** Vigilance choices are made again and again, like committing to going to the gym each day. Remember that one of our key habit-changing strategies is making automated one-off choices so you don't have to make them very often. What can you turn into a one-off? Some of the busiest people we know ensure that they find time for recreation by firm commitments. A colleague of ours, a school principal, takes tap-dancing lessons and is in a hiking group so that she can't back out of these favorite pursuits. Consider, for example, how instead of wishing "I want quality time with my kids," you could make a one-off choice by signing up for a parent-child class.

4. **Identify top device stressors.** Think about which parts of your mobile device use are most stressful for you. If it's reading the news or checking work email, for example, reserve these tasks for times when they won't interfere with relationships. This way, you have your own time and space to process the information rather than interrupting time with those you care about who may react to your negative emotions with their own negativity.

5. **Foster responsibility and cooperation.** Do you tend to "just do it" because colleagues may not follow through or because it's faster to just do it yourself? Or do you hesitate out of guilt to ask for help at home? Yes, it may take a while for others to learn to do it as fast as you might finish, but the long-term space you gain for your true priorities is worth it. Leave room for the on-ramp. You have to change not only your own habits but also those of others who have learned to expect you will do it all!

Five Learning Community Leadership Pathways to Support Balancing Priorities

1. **Create collegiality.** Knowing colleagues isn't fluff. Build it into professional development time. Yes, some activities truly are a waste of time; if you can't identify the purpose in an icebreaker game or discussion question, find something else. People who know what they have in common, be it hobbies or family situations or aspirations or volunteer activities or reading interests, know more about how to reach out and support each other.

2. **Remember the concept of "slack."** It's a fact that many schools plan more than teachers can actually do. That makes balancing priorities tougher than it should be. The 40-hour work week came from Henry Ford experimenting—he got more cars built in five 8-hour days than six 10-hour days. Think about not just how long will it take but also how much bandwidth it will eat up.

   Leaders who strive to reach their vision ensure they have a firm grasp of the reality in which people are operating. Ask someone you trust whether you overestimate what can be done in the time teachers have. Ponder what this means for collective efficacy. Consider whether some priorities need to wait. Remember, the word *priority* didn't have a plural form until the Industrial Revolution.

3. **Model rest and recreation.** Talk about how you engage in the practices this chapter encourages. Encourage teachers to share ideas.

4. **Foster good vibrations.** Review the research on group contagion. Researchers have likened the contagion of moods, concerns, beliefs, and more to the spread of infectious diseases. Pay attention to the moods being spread, and actively use shared values to keep the focus on the good being done in your learning community. We are profoundly affected by the mood around us.

   For example, what is the vibe of your staff lounge? It may be the perfect place to connect. It may be too far away from classrooms for many teachers to visit on short lunch hours. It may be a hotbed of complaints or windowless and depressing. Encourage alternatives. One group of teachers whose rooms were fairly close together decided to lunch together. They vowed to bring healthy food and keep conversations positive. They shared highlights from home and their classrooms so they could get to know one another. They agreed they could ask for advice such as "Who's got a faster way to collect student work?" However, they wouldn't air complaints. And, if one of them *did* have an issue for which they needed support, they knew one another well enough to provide it. Thus, they made their lunch hours recreational.

5. **Commend and appreciate others.** Remember to
   - Thank someone for their contribution.
   - Tell someone something you like about them.
   - Tone down the competition. For instance, in basketball, sometimes players will be so bent on pulling in a rebound that they are fighting their own teammates. In the heat of the moment, a player will yell, "Same team! Same team!" to break up the struggle.

Bandwidth Band Discussion Guide

1. What else have you read that supports the importance of clarifying your priorities? What insights can you share about your priorities and how you are nurturing them?
2. What has held you back from fully supporting your most important priorities?
3. Two of the survey questions in this section are directly affected by the norms and attitudes in your learning community. What evidence have you seen of healthy and unhealthy attitudes toward these two bandwidth factors? What might bring healthier norms to your community?
   - I make sure I take time for rest when I am ill.
   - I take advantage of opportunities to maintain relationships with my coworkers.

6

Filtering Through Possibilities

From the Bandwidth Survey

_____ I monitor my internet surfing (researching information, images, travel arrangements, etc.) so that the time I spend is warranted by the decision I am making.

_____ I have strategies to filter information that allow me to quickly choose among a few high-quality options and arrive at a satisfactory decision.

_____ I can concentrate without being interrupted by worries about schedule/dieting/finances etc.

_____ I avoid "decision fatigue" by automating some decisions (e.g., where I shop or what networking events I attend) to have more energy for others.

_____ I find time to follow my own creative pathways for learning, research, and problem solving.

Curiosity Creator

Before you read this chapter, picture walking through an art street fair, a home or boat show, or a Middle Eastern souk. The souk shops are endless. Much of the merchandise is nearly the same. The shop owners call out, "Step inside here! Come in! Come in!" How would you approach a day at the bazaar? How would you feel at the end of a day of shopping?

The Paradox of Information

We live in the information age. If you type the term into a search engine, you'll get over 5 billion hits in just half a second. If you search for "information filtering techniques," you'll get 100 million hits in the same amount of time. Yes, in this age of abundant information, even learning how to narrow down what might be important is overwhelmingly time-consuming.

Our lives are significantly more complex than even five years ago. We need to pay attention to far more information sources to do our jobs, to learn, to parent, or even to be entertained. Our seemingly distracted state and our endless flitting from one thing to another is not necessarily a sign of disaster, but it is an unconscious adaptation to this current environment. Google is not making us dumber. Instead, we need to web browse intelligently and with agility to remain alert to the next important new thing. We therefore need a real-time system of filters upon filters in order to operate in the explosion of options the internet created.

The Perils of Filtering

The information explosion came with many helpful filters; however, we need to understand how they work so that we don't end up narrowing our choices in unintended or even harmful ways. Internet searches put the world's knowledge at our fingertips, and with that we receive misinformation, incomplete information, one-sided information, and other potential pitfalls. If we aren't careful, using the web reinforces our own cognitive biases.

Particularly worrisome is confirmation bias. Artificial intelligence algorithms bring up items that match your click history. If you aren't careful, you'll only get part of the story; one has to use search terms carefully to avoid this.

Then there's the fact that humans in general try to reserve brain power. Giunti and Atkins (2020) found that people tend to dislike having too much information. They therefore employ filters to find digestible, easy-to-read sources. Usually, that means sticking to familiar ones, which decreases the variety of viewpoints they see, the depth of information they explore, and the quality of their decisions.

To sum up, we *have* to filter, but filtering unwisely has consequences. How do you do it well so that your brain bandwidth doesn't get drained?

The Promises of Filtering

Used well, filters buy back time, attention, and peace of mind. Yes, having the variety of choices the information age makes available feeds our basic needs for autonomy and uniqueness, but in his book *The Paradox of Choice,* Barry Schwartz (2004) captures why filters are so important: having too many choices makes us miserable. His opening story of buying new jeans clearly illustrates his big message. Regular? Slim fit? Boot cut? Relaxed? Skinny? Classic? High-rise? Mid-rise? Distressed? Faded? Have you experienced this? Do you wish you could shop with one of our colleagues who can, with one look, tell you which brand, style, and size will fit you best? *That's* the promise of a good filter. It makes the number of choices manageable and helps you appropriately allocate the amount of time the decision at hand warrants.

Being aware of this paradox helps you value your attention more and understand how filters give you more control over what captures your attention. In his book *The Inevitable,* Kevin Kelly (2016) describes filtering as one of 12 technological forces that will shape our future. He points out that, without crafting our filters, we're letting others dictate what commands our attention.

> Yet for being so precious, our attention is relatively inexpensive. It is cheap, in part, because we have to give it away each day. We can't save it up or hoard it. We have to spend it second by second, in real time. (p. 176)

Ask yourself, "Am I valuing my attention, which I'm giving away for free, as much as advertisers and entertainers and merchants do? Or am I giving it away with no thought to what it costs me?"

The Impact of Maximizing or Satisficing

Making it even more difficult for some of us to count the cost is our hard-wired preference for how much information feels like enough. Even before the internet increased the need for filtering, Herbert Simon won a Nobel Prize in economics for discovering that we don't usually try to maximize decisions by ensuring we've identified the optimal best. Instead, we make the best one we can with the information we have. He coined the term "satisficing" (think *satisfy* and *suffice*) to describe these acceptable yet not optimal choices, contrasting these with "maximizing," where we go much further in exhausting opportunities (Simon, 1947).

Do you tend to maximize or satisfice? Take a look at these descriptions to consider which best matches your approach to decisions.

1. It's worth putting in the time to research options so that you know you've chosen from among the best possible. If I don't spend enough time searching the internet, visiting stores, or asking opinions of others, I'd wonder if I found the best option. Sometimes even when I've done the research and made a purchase, I find myself still evaluating it if new information pops up and looking over my shoulder with potential "buyer's remorse." (Maximizing)

2. It's worth defining "good enough" so that you can end your search as soon as possible. If it meets your criteria and standards (e.g., fit, quality, and price for clothing; image clarity and fit for a presentation image; any latte as long as the shop is on the way to work and allows use of travel mugs), why search further? Yes, another option may exist, but if you stop searching, you'll never know. (Sastisficing)

Can you see how a natural inclination for maximizing can make you more vulnerable to spending more time looking at possibilities than you intended? Choices are attractive, but too many choices require extra brain energy to identify nuanced differences. Also, searching for the optimal result can lead to dissatisfaction because of the fear that you didn't find the best option, even though the difference may be minimal.

Coming back to the paradox of choice, when do you wish to intentionally maximize or satisfice? When for you, personally, are more choices the better path? In either mode, the right filters let you buy back time by ensuring you see the best choices for you in a world that can show you dozens of varieties of almost anything! You'll have more time with friends, for family, for leisure, and for more bandwidth.

Avoiding Decision Fatigue

Too many options can lead to decision fatigue. This occurs when we make multiple decisions during the day without adequately refueling our brain energy. The phenomenon can and does occur in even the most rational individuals. The brain simply wears out. The more choices you make throughout the day, the harder each one becomes. Acting impulsively or doing nothing are often the consequences. The term was first documented by the social psychologist Roy F. Baumeister (Baumeister & Tierney, 2011) to describe the mental and emotional strain resulting from the burden of making choices.

You may have experienced this at a restaurant. Choosing between soup or salad is easy. But as you have to decide the type of dressing, which two of five sides, between baked or mashed, grilled or fried, rare or medium, and mayo or aioli or barbeque sauces, you might default to "Just give me what everyone else is having." Or perhaps at a car dealership, you've exhausted your brain deciding on make, model, year, and trim kit, and the sales rep easily talks you into several other extras you would have nixed a few hours earlier.

The recommendation to never go grocery shopping while hungry is based in research on decision fatigue. The relationship between low glucose levels and decision fatigue was accidentally discovered through a failed experiment at the Baumeister lab. The brain is better at avoiding decision fatigue when adequately supplied, deriving its energy from glucose, the sugar obtained from a wide variety of foods. Researchers at Baumeister's lab tested the impact of glucose on participants and found that supplying glucose helped individuals mitigate loss of self-control and sometimes completely reversed it. With willpower restored via glucose, people exhibited better self-control and made better decisions (Baumeister & Tierney, 2011).

Decision fatigue can also be the result of poor delegation. If all decisions have to go through you, chances are that decision fatigue can creep in. At its worst, people stop making decisions altogether, a phenomenon referred to as decision avoidance.

Good routines are an excellent way to avoid decision fatigue. President Obama found that routinizing mundane aspects of life freed up time for the demands of the office. "You'll see I wear only gray or blue suits. . . . I'm trying to pare down decisions. I don't want to make decisions about what I'm eating or wearing. Because I have too many other decisions to make" (Lewis, 2012).

Can you see how only wearing black turtlenecks like Steve Jobs, ordering the same hot beverage every time you're at a coffee shop, eating the same breakfast, and other routines can help you avoid decision fatigue? Of course, teachers don't want to fall into the trap of the middle school math instructor whose students informed him, "You're wearing your Wednesday shirt on a Tuesday." But saving that decision energy for the right times and issues buys back time and bandwidth.

Researchers (Klein, 2021) estimate that teachers make more than 1,500 decisions a day! Think of all the decisions you make about students, assignments, communications, lessons, and more. If you haven't mentally refreshed yourself, are you ready for evening decisions in your personal life? Think about how often you bend rules—or refuse to bend them—if your children want more screen time or hope to attend a questionable social event. What about the food you eat or order? Do you make poor evening decisions when online shopping? Do you have any maladaptive habits that decision fatigue makes worse? Pay attention and allow for some slack time before deciding.

Curation as a Powerful Filter

One way to filter is through curation, which is simply finding or creating and organizing collections. Think of collaborative resources such as common assessments or lesson plans, or websites you've identified as sources of high-quality supplementary materials. Kelly (2016) lists curation as another essential force of technology. Has your learning community found useful common formats and digital spaces that make sharing lessons worthwhile? The wrong formats can lead to compliance rather than creativity in collaborative planning, or they can lead to lost items or dusty shelves if no one knows what is there. Two great curation tools for filtering possibilities are building lists of the best web resources and using group chats to spread what's working to those interested.

One example of a key resource that decreases time spent on the web is Jane's favorite mathematics site, https://nrich.maths.org. This single site lets you search for rich math tasks by topic, grade level, and difficulty. Lesson plans, implementation suggestions, and samples of student work are included. The problems range from word problems to games to online tasks. It's one-stop-shopping for kindergarten through calculus. Other sites that curate robust lessons include www.rethinkingschools.org and www.learningforjustice.org for across-the-curriculum lessons on equity and collaboration skills. When you find sites like these, you've found a permanent filter for useful materials.

Then, consider using group chats to spread the word. Members of your learning community can add their names to a group chat focused only on sharing stellar resources such as these. Each member only posts the best of the best so that together you've curated a few high-quality sites that meet your needs. You can also notify each other of new shared lesson plans. When you only receive texts from the lesson planning group chats, you get a double filter of fewer texts about better resources!

A Few More Personal Filters

Besides curation, satisficing, and avoiding decision fatigue, here are a few other ways to create or make helpful filters.

- **Have clear criteria in mind** when making choices. For instance, if you were buying a new refrigerator, what are the most important features that you want? Ann, who loves possibilities, found herself looking at dozens and dozens of appliances before reminding herself that filtered water was her top criterion. It is easy to go off the trail if you don't know your destination. Or, if it's movie night, agreeing on whether length or genre or rating is most important can make for a much faster choice. These are simple examples; clarifying criteria, though, takes options off the table quickly.
- **Set a timeline** for making decisions whenever several options would work just fine for you. Ask yourself if there really is only one right answer. Your search for the perfect answer or solution comes with corresponding costs of time and mental bandwidth.
- **Match time invested** with the significance of the decision. Have you seen a colleague experiment as much with the font for an online presentation as with the content? Or choose a motel as if they were choosing a house?

Remember, you're taking the time to set up filters so you have more time for other priorities, including the crucial priority of pursuing creativity.

Choosing to Be Creative

Yes, filtering can buy back time for being creative—for tackling those interests and ideas you never seem to find time to pursue. Know that engaging in creative pursuits energizes the brain, adding to bandwidth. Heather Stuckey and Jeremy Nobel (2010) extensively reviewed the literature on the benefits of creative pursuits and health. They assert that there are clear indications that creative engagement has significantly positive effects on health, including improved focus, less moodiness, faster healing, and more time spent in a state of flow. Thus, when you take time for creative thinking, you are helping your brain function optimally. In fact, creativity is a human universal, meaning that creativity is seen across world cultures. Likewise, creative thinking helped us advance our civilization. When you see a robust indicator of a cross-cultural phenomenon, you can be assured it was baked into our DNA for survival! Hence creativity is essential for our best thinking.

Perhaps you keep putting off your artistic, culinary, crafty, musical, theatrical, or other personal interests. Or, perhaps you wish you had more time to add creative touches to instruction or leadership. Teacher creativity is positively related to student achievement (Rinkevich, 2011).

Does creativity seem like a luxury at work when just getting through curriculum can be overwhelming? Or does the risk of rough patches as you try things for the first time discourage you? What about at home, where all kinds of practical tasks await? David Goldstein and Otto Kroeger (2013) suggest that you give yourself a creative license—literally. Print one up and put it by your desk. They emphasize that we underapply the arts, a travesty when you consider the musical talent and dedication of contributors such as violinist Albert Einstein and Ladytron keyboardist Mira Aroyo, who discovered how bacteria share genetic information. Goldstein and Kroeger point out:

> Even seemingly routine jobs have plenty of new problems to solve and new situations to deal with; there are always improvements that can be made to the process. And unlike other disciplines studied in school, we see through the arts that problems have more than one solution—and many times no right or wrong answers. (p. xxiii)

You are an artist. The students you serve deserve the benefits of your unique creative talents, especially given that no new class of students is quite like the last class you taught, no year proceeds quite the same as any other, and the possibilities for innovation are endless.

American educator Nel Noddings (2013) makes a great case for teacher creativity: how can we expect teachers to encourage and foster creativity in students if the tyranny of standardized curriculum and testing tamps down creativity in teachers?

Justin Berg's research illustrates how easy it is to enter a creative mode. He wanted people to identify new, useful, and novel ideas rather than default to conventional choices. Mimicking a technique often used by managers, he had one group of participants take six minutes to identify three criteria by which they would judge ideas for new products. Their track record was 51 percent for choosing the best new ideas. However, a different use of those six minutes increased that percentage to over 77 percent of the time.

> All it took was having them spend their initial six minutes a little differently: instead of adopting a managerial mindset for evaluating ideas, they got into a creative mindset by generating ideas themselves. Just spending six minutes developing original ideas made them more open to novelty, improving their ability to see the potential in something unusual. (Grant, 2016, p. 43)

Try a bit of this kind of brainstorming before checking what you have curated or evaluating your top choices; you, too, may see more innovative possibilities. And, for your creative endeavors that have nothing to do with work, you're still fueling your brain in ways that benefit your students. You will still have more bandwidth available.

Blameless Discernment Moment

Take a moment to consider which opportunities, tasks, or decisions suck you into the dense black hole of too many possibilities. What is the impact of those drawn-out forays on you, your students, your colleagues, your personal life and those you share it with, and your overall bandwidth? In what areas might adding filters be worthwhile to buy back your valuable time and attention?

Five Individual Pathways for Filtering Possibilities

1. **Quick-start sort.** If you're contemplating several possibilities, do an initial sort. Separating choices into *yes, no,* and *maybe* is a great way to manage options. Writing choices on scrap paper and sorting into physical piles often leads to different thinking as you literally set some choices aside.

2. **Use "good enough."** Look back at the section on satisficing and employ the "good enough" strategy. For what 20 percent of your searches or decisions is maximizing better than satisficing? Can others make some decisions for you? For example, Jane and two other educators dined together after a long day at a conference. We gave our waiter a couple of guidelines and then let him decide what we were going to eat. The result was a series of delicious surprises.

3. **Set a timer.** If you tend to get lost on the internet searching for a lesson idea or the perfect restaurant for the weekend, set a timer. How much of your attention is this search worth?

4. **Automate a choice.** Consider where you, like President Obama, can buy time by automating choices. Perhaps the ultimate example was Steve Jobs and one brand of black turtleneck. One teacher, for example, limited her school wardrobe to quirky skirts and simple tops she found at a neighborhood consignment store. She simply didn't shop in other stores; if they didn't have what she needed, she waited.

5. **Find your experts.** For example, Jane is connected with several language arts teachers on GoodReads.com. If she's hearing a lot of buzz about a new children's or young adult book title, she checks the reviews of these trusted teachers before deciding whether to add it to her reading list.

Five Learning Community Leadership Pathways to Support Filtering Possibilities

1. **Organize specialization.** No one can keep up with everything. For example, your school might organize who filters new options for math instruction, new novels, student discussion techniques, and so on.

During the COVID-19 pandemic, one team of 1st grade teachers designated one person to develop read-alouds and another to research a set of useful virtual math manipulatives. Not only did they trust each other, but they also valued their own time enough to commit to using what the others discovered.

2. **Filter for staff.** What information are leaders passing on to staff, covering in professional development, adding to observation criteria, using for data-driven decisions, and so on? Get some heuristics in place (i.e., priorities, rules of thumb), such as what will have the most impact on students. Jane frequently condenses important research into short readings for professional learning community discussion. They don't have the need or the time to plow through original papers when only about 10 percent of the information is pertinent to them.

3. **Collaborate for filtering.** The pandemic led to more collaboration and less "I should be able to figure this out on my own." Key to fostering this is allowing experts to arise. Who is the go-to for useful picture books, kitchen table science, group-worthy math problems, ways to tie current event assignments to standards, great exit tickets, and other instructional resources?

4. **Identify high-impact and low-impact decisions.** This is similar to the 80/20 strategy for individuals, only it has broad effects for the organization. For example, one school leadership team made the high-impact decision to focus professional development on rich student discussions that involved reasoning and justification. This is a top equity strategy that accelerates learning (Corwin Visible Learning+, n.d.). Then, they left the low-impact decision up to the committee and let them choose the exact topic they would use to introduce techniques.

5. **Identify key decision guidelines.** As you make high-impact decisions, consider the criteria you use or the values in play. Use those to spell out guidelines for others within the organization to make decision making easier. Criteria might include a subset of time needed, expenses, staff enthusiasm, expected impact for the effort, and so on. Sometimes, a simple four-quadrant model looking at impact (high or low) and effort (high or low) can help clarify the importance of the

decision. For example, installing a water fountain that accommodates water bottles may take little effort but have a high impact on staff well-being.

Bandwidth Band Discussion Guide

1. Look back at something you spent entirely too much time doing, from searching for the perfect addition to a lesson plan or professional development session to exploring what might be the best television series to stream next. What, in retrospect, would you do differently?
2. What compels you to keep researching or looking for additional options when making a decision?
3. Pause your discussion and take two minutes to contemplate the following. If you consulted an older, wiser version of yourself, what guidance would he or she give you about evaluating choices and making decisions? What is most important at the end of the day? Share insights with each other. What do you wish to remember about finding the right possibilities without getting lost in the search?

7

Focus Through Mental Habits

From the Bandwidth Survey

_____ I have regular meditation or yoga or journal or other reflective practices.

_____ I avoid multitasking.

_____ I use power naps to clear my mind.

_____ I set aside uninterruptible blocks of time of at least 50 minutes to work on projects that require deep concentration.

_____ I attend to emails at set times rather than constantly.

Curiosity Creator

Try this—please don't just read about it!

1. Pull up the stopwatch on your phone or other device. Draw two horizontal lines on a piece of paper.

2. Time yourself on the following tasks:
   • On the first line, write "It is easy for me to multitask."
   • On the second line, write out the numbers 1–20 sequentially.

3. Now, let's multitask. Draw two more horizontal lines and again set your stopwatch. This time, write a letter on one line and then a number on the line below, then the next letter in the sentence on the upper line, and then the next number in the sequence, changing from line to line (see Figure 7.1). How long did it take to complete the two lines? What surprised you about the experience?

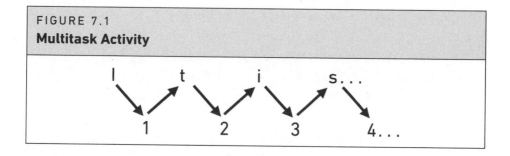

FIGURE 7.1
Multitask Activity

Where Did Attention Spans Go?

I am expected to respond to email, chat, text, phone, and in-person communications immediately, regardless of whether I am mentally invested in another task. Putting off a reply is not considered acceptable.

—School Administrator

Being able to focus your attention for about 52 minutes and then pausing for a 17-minute break appears to be the ideal work pattern for productivity, creativity, and critical thinking (Gifford, 2019). So, when did you last work for close to 52 minutes without being interrupted? Without checking your phone? Without stopping to see if you have the ingredients on hand for dinner? Without pausing to look up a fact or follow some connection your mind is making?

Most educators admit that it's been a long time. In fact, many teachers and administrators report that they're expected to respond quickly to emails, parent calls, and other urgent matters, often at the expense of important work such as providing student feedback, which takes concentration.

If you've been around several decades, you remember the days before people felt scattered and frustrated by the need to always be "on." We do like to blame our technology for our decline in focus. It's definitely part of the problem!

To be fair, though, cellphones (and technology) have also had a positive effect on our lives. A 2018 British TV commercial from Three UK phone service amusingly depicts how cellphones could have changed the course of history. The *Titanic* crew could have known about the iceberg, Henry VIII could have used a dating app to find a new wife, the caveman could have ordered out when food was scarce, and Moses could have filmed the parting of the Red Sea for all to see. Cellphones are *not* bad, they assert.

At the end of the day, technology is both good and bad. As we've mentioned, its emergence in our lives came without strategies to manage it well; we developed our habits in response to new technology rollouts. There is no question that it has had a profound impact on our ability, and that of our students, to focus.

You've probably had at least one conversation regarding "My students simply can't focus! Give them rich text and they lose track of what they're reading before they get through one paragraph!" To drive home the point that not only students are losing focus, in workshops we ask adults to turn their focus to their own reading habits. We give them the opening paragraphs of an award-winning novel written in the 1990s and one written just a couple years ago. We ask them to monitor their focus and engagement with the texts. The results? Almost all say, "The 1990s text is only at an 8th grade level? I can't believe how hard I'm struggling to focus on it!" In contrast, they have no trouble concentrating on the 2016 text, but they are rather chagrined to learn it is written at a 2nd grade level.

Maryanne Wolf, director of the Center for Reading and Language Research and author of *Reader, Come Home,* experimented on herself to check her capacity to focus by rereading a favorite novel, *The Glass Bead Game* by Herman Hesse. She reported, "It was a rather disquieting and actually emotional experience for me . . . I couldn't do it anymore . . . I couldn't slow my reading down to really allocate sufficient attention to what is basically a very difficult and demanding book!" (Zomorodi, 2017, p. 277).

Part of the problem is simply how we are being asked to perform—to be constantly available. But part is the role that technology plays in our lives. Chris Bailey (2016), author of *The Productivity Project,* realized that he was becoming less productive in spite of his expertise on the subject.

> I started to notice my own increased distraction, especially as I accumulated more devices. I had never been so busy while accomplishing so little. I had grown restless with boredom and a lack of stimulation and was trying to cram as much into every moment as

I could. I knew that my brain never functioned well when I was trying to multitask, but I felt compelled to do it anyway. Working with my email client open and my smartphone on my desk was simply more appealing than trying to concentrate on one or two simple things. (p. 3)

Does that sound familiar? Let's look first at why this kind of multitasking doesn't match how our brains work and then at what to do about it!

The Truth About Multitasking

Through this chapter's Curiosity Creator, you just experienced trying to multitask, attempting to complete two seemingly simple endeavors that when combined take far more time and energy. Yes, you can grade papers while listening to music or walk and listen to a podcast. In these cases, one task is already automatic—it doesn't require any prefrontal cortex activity. But multitasking involving two tasks that require your attention isn't actually multitasking—it's task switching, which leads to one or more activities being compromised.

Your brain on multitasking is like a computer with several windows open: you're compromising efficiency and speed. Brain scientist John Medina (2014), in his book *Brain Rules*, reports that task switching results in 50 percent more errors and increases the time it takes to complete tasks by more than 50 percent. In our workshops, most people who try the exercise at the start of this chapter find this to be true.

Not only that, but task switching is among the quickest ways to deplete brain energy. Remember that the prefrontal cortex (PFC) occupies approximately 10 percent of the brain by volume but requires a disproportionate amount of energy to function. This is due to the complexity of the tasks the PFC is responsible for, including planning, memory, flexibility, inhibition, and initiation. Each time you switch tasks, your PFC acts as a switchboard to recruit neurons from the appropriate areas of your brain to engage. Each time you interrupt one task and start another—even such simple switches as alternating writing numbers and letters—this switchboard process begins anew. Down go effectiveness, efficiency, and energy.

Compounding the draining effects of multitasking is the effort required to refocus. Gloria Mark, who researches digital distraction at the University of California–Irvine, discovered that after an interruption, it takes over 23 minutes to fully regain focus on your original task (Mark, Wang, & Niiya, 2014).

Much of our multitasking seems so benign, yet its consequences are far-reaching. Do we really want to lose our capacity to think deeply? And how can we require it of students if we're failing at it ourselves? Let's focus on regaining the time we're losing to interruptions, temptations, and task switching.

Assessing Your Focus

If you're thinking, "I can just bury my phone. That'll let me concentrate," know that researchers found that even having your phone out of sight but close by can affect focus and learning. Tanil and Yong (2020) found that even thinking about your phone has a negative effect on learning and memory. Phones and focus don't mix well.

Sometimes you can find motivation for changing habits via a little data collection. Try one of the following:

- Count how many times a day you check your phone. Compare data for a weekday and a weekend day. Free apps such as "Moment—Screen Time Control" will count for you, as will screen time settings on newer phones. According to a survey by Deloitte (2018), Americans check their smartphones about 52 times a day.

- Consider counting how often you're on your device when in the presence of those most important to you. Remember the impact that mobile device usage has on relationships.

- Check how long you are working on your computer, laptop, or tablet without interrupting yourself. Mark et al. (2014) showed that the most productive workers interrupted themselves every 75 seconds when working in front of a screen. Given that we optimally work for 52 minutes at a stretch, as mentioned above, there is incredible potential for improving our focus, efficiency, and engagement!

- Monitor how long you concentrate when reading complex texts. Pick up a favorite literary novel from years ago, a classic, or a research article. How long can you read before you find your mind elsewhere? How long do you wish you could read before being distracted?

- Track your work week. How many times did you succeed in focusing on a complex task for the optimal 52 minutes without interruption? Examples include giving feedback on student writing (or on teaching strategies if you are a coach or administrator), employing backward planning in creating units, planning for student engagement, or reviewing data for patterns.

Now, given these, take time to reflect. Where do you need to gain focus? What "Name the Gain" goal would help you increase your focus for the tasks that require it?

Let's look at a few ways to get there.

Pathways for Regaining Focus

Focus is one area where we can be thankful for neuroplasticity. Yes, new digital habits and the pace of life have decreased focus, but new habits can restore your ability to focus deeply and for optimal periods of time. All are relatively simple and inexpensive to implement, yet they all take conscious effort. We'll look first at why these work and then at strategies for forming new habits with them.

To Sleep, Perchance to Focus

If you haven't noticed, the desire to close your eyes often competes with your desire to focus on complex tasks. This is why factor analysis, a statistical technique that finds how items cluster together, placed the question "I use power naps to clear my mind" in this section of the Bandwidth Survey. Most of the information on sleep is in Chapter 8, but naps are so undervalued in the culture of education (not even kindergartners get them anymore) that we want to mention a few things here.

Because our societal focus is on staying awake, people have lost track of the amazing restorative power of short naps. If you're going to engage in critical tasks, such as influencing the lives of children, you need to be alert. Know that a NASA study (Stickgold, 2009) on sleepy military pilots and astronauts found that a 40-minute nap improved performance by 34 percent and alertness by 100 percent. Who do you want piloting your plane? Or teaching your child?

Power naps will not overcome sleep deprivation (more on that in Chapter 8), but if you feel the pull of drowsiness as you sit down to complete a task, know that rather than powering through for 60 minutes to get it done, taking that 17-minute catnap and *then* concentrating for 43–52 minutes will let you get more done.

And how does a teacher find time for a power nap? It may just be the best use of your lunch hour on some days. No scientific evidence shows that any drug, such as caffeine, or technique, such as loud music or splashing cold water on your face, can take the place of sleep in restoring your ability to focus (Walker, 2017).

Mindfulness and Focus

Many learning communities have adapted mindfulness training and provide opportunities to engage in the practice as a way for students and adults alike to handle stress. But the benefits of mindfulness flow to other areas as well. According to *The Intelligence Trap* by David Robson (2019), there is strong evidence that, besides the many well-documented health benefits, regular practice of mindfulness can improve your emotional compass—introspection, differentiation, and regulation—meaning that it is the quickest way to de-bias your decision making and hone your intuitive instincts. You're also less apt to fall victim to cognitive biases.

After all, mindfulness helps you focus. No one is naturally good or bad at meditation and mindfulness. It takes practice and an understanding that part of its purpose is to build awareness of when your mind is wandering or on task. Check the section about "Five Pathways for Individuals to Focus Attention" in this chapter for ways to get started, even if meditation bears little attraction for you.

Your Environment and Focus

Remember when "do not disturb" signs meant that closed doors needed to remain closed? Many of us need to ponder how we can create similar spaces where others understand that our current task needs our undivided attention. In some schools, where teachers share office space and find that students or colleagues drop by whenever they try to concentrate in their classrooms, this can take some creativity. It may also take a reexamination of the Care of Self and Care of Others interdependency discussed in Chapter 4. Ask yourself: "For what key activities do I need those uninterrupted blocks of time to concentrate? How much time can I gain back, time that I can give to others, if I first meet my own need for concentration?"

Experiment with blocking out an hour after school one day a week at someplace like your local library, where you can reserve a small study room for free, to tackle that new book and how you might create a lesson around it; to grade assignments that involve higher-level thinking by students; or to look for patterns in data. What happens to your creativity, concentration, and productivity?

One school superintendent discovered it was better to put a sign on his door saying "I'll be ready to chat at 10 a.m." rather than snarling, "What is it now!" if someone took his "open door policy" seriously. In our workshops, we hand out "Brain at Work—Do Not Disturb" doorknob hangers.

Another group of administrators worked together so that each person had one block of time every week to work on complex tasks. They scheduled a day when each administrator had no student discipline responsibilities. They were to use part of that day to squirrel themselves away far from disruptions and concentrate on a complex task.

An instructional coach took the information on finding focus to heart, telling us, "I have made some steps toward this, including downloading a meditation app. In a new position this year, I have not employed some of these strategies that seem simple. For example, as a classroom teacher I checked email before school, during my prep, and after school. As a coach I get to check email all . . . day . . . long. I am looking forward to time-blocking those tasks. It just never occurred to me."

A Final Thought

Note that focusing your attention doesn't mean being productive every moment of the day. A better way to think of it is, is your mind where you want it to be? If you need downtime on a Saturday morning, focusing on your current binge-watch show means you're focused. If your goal is to listen to your students' ability to build on one another's thoughts, can your mind stay on what they are saying? If you're relaxing with a good thriller, detective story, fantasy epic, or hobby magazine rather than complex text, that's OK unless you meant to use the time to read deeper text.

In summary, ponder how often you're choosing how to focus your attention, your ability to do so, and whether you're able to follow through when you intend to focus.

Blameless Discernment Moment

What are your current strategies for staying focused? What is most likely to distract you? Rate your ability to focus on a scale of 1–10, with 10 being your optimal capacity.

Now, instead of wallowing in despair over your current self-rating, define a simple step you know you can take toward incremental improvement. If you rated yourself a *3*, what might you do to reach a *4*? If you're a *5*, what would take you to a *6*, and so on? Be careful not to blame yourself ("I'm so scattered!"), others ("They keep interrupting me!"), or circumstances ("How can I focus with so much chaos around here?!"). Like the captain of a ship, you're using your best strategies to get to your destination given the current conditions.

Five Pathways for Individuals to Focus Attention

1. **Meditate.** Basic meditation is a form of mind training that increases your capacity to stay focused. Concentrating on one thing, usually breath, develops awareness of when your mind is unfocused. Start with 5 minutes a day and work up to 20 minutes.

   One of our favorite first steps for meditation can be found at www .positiveintelligence.com/resources/. Scroll down to "PQ Gym" and try the 5-minute or 15-minute meditations.

   You'll find strategies for mindful eating in Chapter 8. Note that you can also employ mindfulness during a workout. Yes, you might focus on breathing. Or you can pay attention to what your muscles are doing as you strike a yoga pose or lift a weight. Or you can concentrate on the feeling of the pavement or dirt path as you walk or run.

Another alternative is putting on a favorite tune and listening with your eyes closed, perhaps isolating one instrument or voice for your undivided attention. Mindfulness can be fun!

2. **Take a nap!** Try a nap to refresh your brain. The key is to truly nap without fear of oversleeping. Both of us use the Sleep Cycle Power Nap app, which allows you take naps of approximately 20, 45, or 90 minutes in length, gently waking you with music at approximately the right moment—before you go into too deep a sleep—based on your body movements. Phone alarms also work. Just make sure not to jolt yourself awake!

3. **Avoid interruptions.** What do you need to do to avoid interrupting yourself? Plan for at least one 60-minute time block to go "old school" and experience the benefits of flow when working. While it may not be possible to achieve this during certain parts of the school day, look for opportunities to leverage this practice.

4. **Disable notifications.** Emails and other electronic notifications are designed to be addicting. And it's easy to rationalize that we must always be available. Challenge that theory by expanding the time between checking for new emails. Discover your optimal balance between availability and uninterrupted focus. Consider putting an automatic reply in place for your email to let important individuals such as parents know that in the interest of focusing on quality teaching for their children, emails will be addressed during set times of the day.

5. **End multitasking.** Multitasking (i.e., task switching) can often be remediated by developing awareness around multitasking habits. Task switching is among the most draining activities for the brain, so there is a substantial payoff for staying on task when possible.

Often, we task switch when something suddenly occurs to us that needs to be done.

Try "offloading" before you begin a task by keeping a running list nearby to record new thoughts of important yet not urgent tasks. This takes away the worry that you might forget the thought. Bailey (2018) calls these "open loops" and reminds us that it takes energy to ignore them, draining your precious bandwidth. Are you a worrier? Or do you want to hold onto a great idea not related to the task at hand? Or might you suddenly remember you promised to stop by the grocery store? Keep a notebook open for these "distractions lists" so you can close these loops and refocus, and then deal with them later.

Five Learning Community Leadership Pathways to Support Focusing Attention

1. **Use the research.** Point out how inefficient task switching is. Suggest a new email norm—an automated message stating when during the day you answer emails. Schwartz (2011) reports that even when top executives do this, there are few or no complaints. People adapt to delays if they know how long the delays will be.

2. **Change meeting norms.** If a staff meeting is truly important (and a first step is ensuring that the time is valuable for all who are there), then task switching shouldn't be the norm. Find out what has to happen so that teachers aren't tempted to grade papers or deal with parent communication. For example, ask those you can trust to give honest feedback about why the meeting content doesn't seem valuable. Have a no-phones-out policy or train staff on how to only have vital notifications come through.

3. **Disrupt interruptions.** Now that you understand the dangers of interrupting concentration, consider practices in your building. For what is the public address system used? When do people knock on classroom doors? For example, a principal new to a building discovered that over 80 parents per grade level were bringing forgotten lunches or assignments to the building every day, resulting in interruptions in far too many first-hour classrooms. She placed a set of drawers in the office where parents deposited the items and made students responsible for collecting them during passing time. How else might you systemically eliminate classroom interruptions?

4. **Change what is rewarded.** Productivity isn't linear; tasks expand to fill time allotted, and we slow down as more hours go by. Here are some suggestions for focusing on focus as a school.

- Make sure that teachers are sharing ways they're working smarter, not longer, whether they've found a technology solution or have a tip for concentrating in the midst of the school day. Point out practices that decrease both internal (losing focus yourself) and external interruptions, and highlight the benefits.
- Describe to the whole staff the habitual behaviors that lead to task switching. This decreases individual defensiveness.
- Add a couple of check-in moments at meetings to see if the new strategies for focusing are helping without creating more distractions. Trial and error are important here, as what works for some won't work in the same way for others.
- Honor focus, not task switching, by ensuring, for example, that if there's a moratorium on grading student work during meetings, then the meetings don't rob teachers of time they need to grade papers!

5. **Form new habits together.** Set a challenge to all teachers such as the following and have them use some time in their learning communities to discuss their experience and hone their skills. (Note that teachers might also use variations of these with students.)

- Grade one set of assignments with your smartphone beside you and another with your smartphone at least five cognitive steps away (cognitive steps are explained on in Chapter 3). What happened to your productivity?
- Find one block of 52 minutes to concentrate on a challenging task. In your next learning community meeting, discuss how you protected yourself from interruption and closed "open loops." What happened to your ability to focus?
- Experiment with background noise. Bailey (2018) summarizes research demonstrating that familiar, fairly simple music helps many people concentrate better. And noise-cancelling headphones stop the drain of hearing one side of a conversation (because your brain tries to fill in the other side).
- Consider "Focus Friend" pairings for accountability and support. Perhaps two minutes of a meeting are used for a "turn and talk" about how their focus capacity is developing. Or perhaps the Focus Friends find their own slivers of time, once a week or once a month, to encourage each other and fine-tune strategies.

Bandwidth Band Discussion Guide

1. Come up with an analogous object to describe your typical ability to focus. Are you a laser? A prism? Discuss how you can use your analogy to ensure you are choosing when and on what you will focus.
2. What factors contribute to your ability to focus? Which of the "Form New Habits Together" suggestions might your band use?
3. Give a name to your biggest distractions. Is it the Hunger Monster? Morpheus, the god of sleep? Share with your group. Practice anticipating and using humor to dismiss your distraction, such as "Oh, Hunger Monster, I knew you'd show up, and I'm ready with a nutritious snack that'll devour *you!*"

8

Fueling Your Brain

From the Bandwidth Survey

_____ I exercise regularly.

_____ I make healthy food choices (e.g., balanced diet and my chosen indulgences in moderation).

_____ I get enough sleep. Note: Indicators of insufficient sleep include being overly irritable or moody, craving junk food or caffeine, and struggling to stay alert.

_____ I make sure I have access to water for staying hydrated.

Curiosity Creator

This is a true story. Ann's Aunt Marion grew up on high-fat Polish food, started smoking at age 14, and drank scotch every day. When she was 94, she collapsed at a casino and was taken to a hospital. After a few medical tests, she said, "Enough. Take me home or I will take a cab. I have a party on Friday night." Indeed, they released her, and off to the party she went that Friday night. Saturday morning, she never awakened.

Here's another character to ponder: Teddy Roosevelt. He allegedly drank a gallon of coffee every day, complete with five to seven lumps of sugar in each cup. Teddy died at age 60 from a blood clot in his leg that went to his lungs. However, the decline in health of this president known for physical prowess was largely attributed to a variety of jungle illnesses he contracted a few years earlier while exploring the Amazon River with an ill-fated expedition.

Whenever Ann shares these stories, people voice a wide range of inter-pretations. What is your take on the Aunt Marion story? Or on Roosevelt's robust health—until it deteriorated?

Fueling, Refueling, and Bandwidth

You've heard it all before: exercise, diet, sleep. But have you? Have you inter-nalized how important these are? We can all point to someone we know who powered through their days while violating important health guidelines. With all of the conflicting "expert" suggestions, it can make us throw up our hands and say that no one really knows and none of it matters anyway. While stories like Aunt Marion's and Teddy Roosevelt's are powerful, we really need to focus on general principles that affect most of us, not the outliers. One can't really argue with the fact that our brains need fuel. If your bandwidth "tank" is on empty, you will falter regardless of what focus and filter strate-gies you employ.

We aren't going to attempt a definitive list of perfect diet, sleep, and fit-ness strategies in these few pages. What we will try to do is

- Consolidate the best advice on forming diet, exercise, and sleep hab-its—not what, but how to decide on fueling strategies.
- Summarize the brain research: the reasons that might motivate you to take charge.
- Provide examples of how you can use the key willpower strategies from Chapter 3 to trash any maladaptive habits and craft sustainable approaches to diet, sleep, and fitness.

Remember, bandwidth is about being energized, effective, and engaged, as well as maximizing your emotional intelligence capacity. Bandwidth is essential, not a nice thing when you have time for it. Recognize, though, that society in general can push us away from this realization. In his bestselling book *Essentialism: The Disciplined Pursuit of Less,* Greg McKeown (2014) points out:

> To discern what is truly essential we need space to think, time to look and listen, permission to play, wisdom to sleep, and the discipline to apply highly selective criteria to the choices we make.

Ironically, in a Nonessentialist culture these things—space, listening, playing, sleeping, and selecting—can be seen as trivial distractions. At best they are considered nice to have. At worst they are derided as evidence of weakness and wastefulness. (p. 60)

Please read on with this mindset: "Finding strategies for fueling is essential to my effectiveness, both at school and in my personal life. This is my chance to discover what will truly work for who I am and how I live."

Fueling: Separating Facts and Fiction

Remember that the questions for this section of the Bandwidth Survey are all about the actual fuel our brains need, which is the input we provide: food, beverages, sleep, and exercise. In contrast, the other sections reflect how we use up that energy.

Know that much of what might seem like conflicting advice is actually flowing from new research made possible by advances in neuroscience techniques. Fernando Gómez-Pinilla (2008) summarized discoveries around specific nutrients and how they affect cognitive function. These nutrients often work together with good sleep and exercise habits. This means that specific diet and activity alterations have major potential to improve cognitive function as well as ward off and repair damage to our brains. Note that this also means that many fad diets that do not pay attention to specific nutrients can rob you of these vital dietary components. The base of knowledge has only grown since then.

However, popular media often exaggerates or reports in isolation the results of a study. Thus, filtering your sources to ensure you're receiving wise advice is essential.

One commonly mentioned health strategy is drinking more water, which is the easiest fuel to address. We all know we'll die of thirst before hunger, but dehydration is dangerous long before that most extreme outcome. Nathalie Pross (2017) researched the effects of mild dehydration throughout the lifespan. When children get thirsty and begin to move toward more serious symptoms of dehydration, they get crabby and are less competent with cognitive tasks. Dehydration produces the same mood changes for those in the prime of life but has less impact on brain function. As we age further, dehydration continues to affect mood but, again, impairs cognitive function, with the rate of impairment increasing as we age.

Let's go through the other sources of brain fuel one by one.

Sleep

Sleep isn't merely time spent in bed. Sleep quality is as important as sleep quantity. How we can achieve quality sleep is dependent on a number of factors. The following 12 tips for healthy sleep are suggested by the National Institute of Health (National Library of Medicine, 2012) and Dr. Matthew Walker (2017) in his book *Why We Sleep*.

1. Stick to a sleep schedule.

Going to bed and waking up at the same time each day maintains your circadian rhythm—the timing of the body's internal clock—and sticking to a sleep schedule requires an intentional mindset. Some of the other tips in this list will help you create a routine that prepares your mind and body for rest. Most educators find keeping to such a schedule quite easy Monday through Friday, but they look forward to sleeping in on the weekends. As enticing as that may sound, don't overdo it. Your body can't adjust to a set sleeping routine if your weekend schedule is drastically different from your weekday.

How do you know if you've found a good sleep schedule? Think about how easy it is to get out of bed when the alarm goes off, or how often you awaken before the alarm sounds.

2. Don't exercise too late in the day.

While the next section covers how physical fitness enhances mental fitness, note that some individuals have a difficult time winding down if they exercise too late in the day. If you have no choice but to exercise closer to bedtime, try to finish two to three hours before you plan to hit the sack. Experiment with ways to settle in that will prepare you for sleep. Try a warm bath, yoga, or a cup of chamomile tea.

3. Avoid caffeine, nicotine, and other stimulants.

Colas, coffee, many nonherbal teas (including some green teas), and chocolate contain caffeine, which is a stimulant. These are best consumed before noon as a rule of thumb; it takes about eight hours for caffeine to leave your system. Some individuals will insist that they are not affected by caffeine late in the day. While that is possible, it is more likely that they are used to poorer sleep quality and aren't aware of the difference between their current and desired states. Note that nicotine is also a stimulant. Besides keeping you up past bedtime, nicotine withdrawal can awaken you before you're fully rested. Some dietary supplements, hydration tablets, and other seemingly innocent products also contain stimulants that interfere with quality sleep.

4. Avoid alcoholic drinks before bed.

While a nightcap may seem like a logical way to relax, alcohol is a sedative, robbing you of REM sleep by keeping you in the lighter stages of sleep. Many people wake up when the sedation effects wear off, leading to tossing and turning. Heavy ingestion of alcohol can impair breathing at night, again causing you to wake up.

5. Avoid large meals and beverages late at night.

A light snack before bed is OK, but a heavy meal can cause digestive issues that interfere with sleep. Drinking too many fluids can cause frequent awakenings to urinate. Lying down after a large meal can cause sleep-disruptive digestive reflux.

6. Avoid medicines that delay or disrupt your sleep (where possible).

Some commonly prescribed heart, blood pressure, or asthma medications, as well as some over-the-counter and herbal medicines for coughs, colds, or allergies, can disrupt sleep patterns. If you have trouble sleeping, consider speaking to your doctor or pharmacist to see if any of the drugs you are taking may be contributing to this. It might be possible to take them earlier in the day.

7. Don't nap after 3:00 p.m.

Power naps of 20 minutes or less can be beneficial during the day. However, napping too close to bedtime can result in difficulty falling asleep at night. Experiment with how you time your naps to observe the effects on your ability to sleep well at night. Avoid the cycle of poor nighttime sleep, napping, another poor night's sleep, napping, and so on.

8. Make time to relax before bed.

Instead of packing your evening schedule (especially if you are tempted to grade papers or answer emails after spending the evening with family or friends), work to make time for unwinding before bed. How many of us toss and turn at night, failing to doze off as our minds process our day? Try off-loading those thoughts in a journal and creating your to-do list for the next day before crawling between the covers. Reading also settles the brain, provided that the content isn't anxiety-provoking.

9. Take a hot bath before bed.

After a hot bath, your body temperature drops. This often causes sleepiness, helping you slow down and relax before bed.

10. Have a dark, cool (in temperature), gadget-free bedroom.

We sleep better at night if the temperature in the room is kept on the cool side. The optimal temperature is 65 degrees Fahrenheit (Walker, 2017). Electronic devices such as mobile phones and computers can be a distraction. Turn any clocks away from you if, when insomnia strikes, you find yourself continually checking the time. Also, blue light screens suppress the secretion of melatonin, a hormone that regulates sleep/wake cycles. Usually, melatonin increases in the evening to induce sleep. There are several blue light filters for phones and tablets, including Twilight, f.lux, and Night Light.

11. Get the right sunlight exposure.

Sun exposure during the day helps us regulate sleeping patterns. Try to get outside in the natural sunlight for at least 30 minutes per day. A light therapy alarm clock can also benefit your circadian rhythm. Note, too, that sleep experts recommend a full hour of sunshine in the morning for those who struggle to sleep, as well as turning down lights a few hours before bedtime.

12. Don't stay in bed if you (really) can't sleep.

If you find yourself still awake after 20 minutes in bed or you're starting to get anxious about sleeping well, get up and do something else until you feel sleepy. Trying to force yourself to sleep seldom works. Try forcing yourself to stay awake; paradoxically, this often induces sleep!

Exercise

Exercise is not a luxury; your body was made to move. Working on aerobic fitness, strength, and balance allows us to enjoy so many more aspects of life. Exercise provides the fastest way to boost willpower, increase mental sharpness, bolster resistance to stress, and improve self-control in other aspects of life (Ratey, 2013). Know that even a five-minute walk around the block provides a significant boost in bandwidth.

If you feel like there's a new recommendation every year on the optimal amount of exercise we need, you just may be right. A new study (Reynolds, 2020) indicated that as little as 11 minutes of brisk walking per day can offset the effects of days filled with sitting. Previous studies that suggested up to 60 minutes of exercise was necessary relied on self-reports of movement, whereas this study had people wear activity monitors. We'd suggest setting your sights a bit higher than 11 minutes, but at least this new information means that adequate exercise really is doable! Here are some strategies for finding a plan you'll stick with.

Motivate That Elephant

What's your big why? "I know I'm supposed to exercise" is usually followed by "but. . . ." Here are some big whys others have found motivating.

- I want to be fit enough so I'm not so exhausted by work that I can't enjoy my personal time.
- I want to stay fit so I can walk when I'm 80.
- What I do now will affect whether I can keep up with children—my own, my students, maybe even my grandchildren.
- I want my clothes to fit.

- I want to be able to keep up with the guys during Saturday morning pick-up basketball games. I don't want to be a weekend warrior casualty.
- I want to be a role model for people who are important to me.

Shape the Path

Find the easiest way possible to fit in some exercise. Park as far away as you can from your classroom or office. Take the stairs whenever you can. Combine walking with a meeting, listening to a book you need to read, or . . . television. Heath and Heath (2010) tell of a single mom who was sure she had no time to exercise. They suggested she march in place during commercials as she watched the evening news. Not ideal but very doable. Soon she was marching from the beginning of the first commercial until the end of the second, and then the third. Pretty soon she was up to 30 minutes.

Find Something You Want to Do

Jane happens to like running. Whenever people comment, "I hate running. I just can't get into working out," she tells them, "Then don't run!" She mentions how much she hates strength training yet has friends who can't wait to pick up kettlebells.

Ann loves yoga and walking her dogs. When it's snowy, she enjoys cross-country skiing. Dancing, on the other hand, makes her feel self-conscious, so you won't catch her in a Zumba class.

Everyone has a potential exercise strategy that, once employed, will become so essential that it will feel like something is missing once it becomes a matter of habit. Suzanne Brue, a friend and colleague of ours, researched how people with different personality types prefer to exercise. What were their favorite activities? How did classes, fitness trainers, being in nature, and other factors affect them? At https://the8colorsoffitness.com you can take a quiz, find your "fitness color," and read tips on what just might work for you.

Engage in the Possible Rather Than Pursue the Perfect

Have you heard of the "what the hell" effect? Dieting researchers coined the term in 2010. It might be pie or an open bag of chips or more than a little wine left in the bottle. You've vowed not to have any, then to have only a taste, then a small serving, and then "Oh, what the hell, I've already blown it, so I might as well keep going."

There's no logic to that. You haven't committed a grievous transgression by having a little. You can still feel good about yourself by saying, "I'm not a failure. Slipping a little doesn't doom me, so I'll just stop." You can reach your goals much more quickly by correcting course during small infractions rather than deciding you blew it so you might as well just let it all go.

This can work in a reverse way, too. Perhaps your ideal workout is a class at a gym that's been canceled, a five-mile walk when you only have time for two miles, or circuit training and you're stuck at home with a sick child. Instead of writing it off, settle for less than ideal. Less is still something. Remember, even 11 minutes of brisk walking can make a difference. If you can get to a flight of stairs, a couple of heavy cans, a resistance band, or a chair for certain moves, you can embrace what is possible.

Sit, Stand, Stretch

Capitalize on the importance of balance, strength, and flexibility. All of these help you avoid injury, can be done with the kind of mindfulness that increases bandwidth, and fit well into little chunks of time. Five seconds of web searching produced an excellent starter's guide from www.allactive.co.uk called "Chair-Based Strength Exercises." You might engage in these as you think hard before commenting on a student's work or calm your mind for an after-school team meeting.

Similarly, balance exercises are crucial and compact, with plenty of online resources to get you started. Always check the integrity of the source you're drawing from; not all advice from incredibly fit trainers, for example, is appropriate for those ramping up their exercise program. At www.mayoclinic.org, we found a tutorial called "Introduction to Balance Exercises," some of which you might even engage in with students for an energizing break from mental exercise.

Use Small-Space Gymnasiums

Perhaps one of the gifts of the 2020 pandemic was how many ideas people had for working out in small spaces. People who experienced lockdown in cities where they were expected to remain in their small apartments, leaving only for grocery and essential work, created options and shared them all over social media.

Early on in the pandemic, in an article titled "The Small Space Workout Challenge" (McKeough, 2020), the *New York Times* captured what many fitness experts were doing, complete with photos, guides to inexpensive equipment, ideas for items you already have on hand, tips for not annoying neighbors, and so on. What might work in your living space, your classroom, or the teacher lounge with a couple of colleagues also interested in a fast power workout?

Look for a Virtual Class

Here again, the 2020 pandemic opened up a wide variety of choices. What do you need? Some fitness centers are offering a full menu of classes for reasonable fees. Other trainers are streaming free workouts. Check your health insurance provider website as well; many have added free video classes as part of wellness programs.

For years, Jane and her daughter, a school speech and language pathologist, have been using the "Seven-Day Melt My Muffin Top" core workout they found at https://skinyms.com. Having a variety of rotating exercises through the week is motivating for them. To find other quality programs, search www.businessinsider.com for an updated list of excellent virtual workouts for different purposes. Many were free during the pandemic, including ones from the YMCA and LifeTime Fitness. As with all exercise programs, look for reviews, ask your doctor about any precautions you might take as you try new things, and *listen to your body*. Just know that, whether it's beginning yoga, exercise for seniors, walking-in-place workouts that will get your heart rate up, or Zumba classes, they're out there on the web.

DVD workouts can also be an answer if you need to exercise during off hours or while children sleep or simply don't have access to a good outdoor area. Search "Best Fitness Videos" and you'll find lists that indicate great options for runners, seniors, beginners, and so on. Check your local library, too, for downloadable workout videos to borrow—rotating which ones you use can keep the catchy workout tunes from turning into earworms!

Multitask

Multitask? What? I thought I wasn't supposed to do that. When it comes to behaviors like walking that are well-entrenched in our basal ganglia, we can add another activity such as listening to audiobooks. In fact, Ann only listened to the Harry Potter series when walking. Needless to say, she substantially upped her miles while doing this. Both Jane and Ann enjoy audiobooks with exercise and in fact share audiobooks that spark creative ideas for collaboration. One caveat: always be aware of your surroundings and adjust accordingly.

Another effective way to multitask is holding a walking meeting. Use the smartphone memo feature to capture ideas and decisions. Steve Jobs was known for his walking meetings with clients and colleagues.

Finally, turn fitness time into family time. Jane can speak firsthand of the workout potential of the *Dance Dance Revolution* system, first popularized when her daughter was in middle school. Years ago, Wii Fit took the world by storm. Nothing quite as universal has taken its place, but newer gaming system fitness options include *Just Dance* (with a new release every year), *Ring Fit Adventure,* and *Fitness Boxing.* Ask your students what the newest options are!

Find Apps for Yoga or Other Exercises

The quintessential app for yoga is Yoga Studio. As of this writing, it is $4.99 for the download. The content is regularly updated to include new routines. You can choose from beginner, intermediate, and advanced. The routines are as short as 10 minutes and as long as an hour. You can download certain routines to your phone for when the internet is not available.

Get Out in Nature

The evidence is in: no matter whether it's a small park or garden, wide-open country, or a nearby forest, nature improves our physical and psychological well-being and our ability to focus. An article titled "Nurtured by Nature" (Weir, 2020) cites multiple research findings. While it isn't always possible to take your walk or run or yoga time outside, even just taking a moment during boring tasks to gaze at lovely flowers improved concentration. Being out in nature is shown to buffer the effects of loneliness and isolation, increase feelings of contentment and purpose, and improve overall health and well-being, even if it's just two hours a week. And, as the flower example shows, any time with nature is better than no time. Being outside can multiply your other efforts to improve bandwidth.

Bottom line? No excuses. The elephant rider knows this—and again, the link between healthy body and healthy brain is undisputable. But that elephant is hard to motivate—which "why am I doing this" will work for you? Then, shape your path using at least one of the above options. This is doable and essential to your bandwidth.

We know secondary teachers who bike to work all year long, and that's quite the commitment in Minnesota. Their schools allow teachers to use the gym showers, and they bring clean clothes to change into, tapping into foldable, wrinkle-free wardrobe choices.

One teacher, a former college basketball player, took the time to shoot a few baskets after lunch. This served as an opportunity to exercise as well as clear her head. Another school principal used the exercise equipment at school to get fit. She particularly enjoyed watching the comings and goings outside of the gym window, which made each workout a unique experience!

Food Wants and Needs

And then there's the simple yet complex truth that we are what we eat and drink. No, we aren't going to give advice on gluten or sugar or whatever. We will, however, review a few facts about the effects of certain foods on brain function and share some overarching principles and strategies for fueling with the brain in mind.

Mind the Basics

Yes, nutrition advice is so varied that you just might be able to find support for any crazy fad. However, a few key brain/diet connections are worth internalizing. In her Harvard Health Blog "Nutritional Psychiatry: Your Brain on Food," Dr. Eva Schelb (2020) points out that our brains are like expensive cars that work best with high-quality fuel. That means the more nutritious the food, the better. And, if we use lower-grade "fuel"—overdoing sugars or other junk food—it doesn't have the capacity to cleanse itself of waste that results. She points out that too much refined sugar can harm our brains, interfere with how we regulate insulin, foster inflammation, and even cause mood disorders in some people.

You probably won't be surprised that she and her fellow researchers recommend cutting back on processed foods and sugar; exploring the Mediterranean diet with its omega-3 fatty acids, vegetables, fish; and consuming whole, unprocessed grains. Yes, you'll find endorsements for many, many, *many* other diets, but before trying one . . .

Believe the Experts—After You've Vetted Them

If you haven't noticed, there's a bit of a "you can't trust experts" attitude out there toward diets. Usually the rationale is "Remember? They told us not to eat eggs. They recommended cutting fat from our diets. They were *wrong!*"

A better way to think about these reversals in advice from the experts is "They were learning." In education, we've learned the value of evidence-based practices. We look for practices where good research has demonstrated effectiveness. We move on when research shows better ways, or when emerging practices show solid results even as more vetting is needed. We understand that peer review keeps researchers honest and that paying attention to the environment in which the results were created can help us decide whether or not a practice will work in our own environment.

Let's apply the same principles to nutrition—and help our older students do the same. Yes, you can find support for all kinds of fad diets on the internet. Remember, though, that internet searches are designed to bring up articles that are closely related to articles you just finished reading; if you read an endorsement of the newest "eat this, not that" program, you'll be directed to more of the same. (The Netflix documentary *The Social Dilemma* explains how the search engines work and is well worth watching.)

Rather than trusting people you know or opinions from those who stand to profit from your choices, start by considering any program with general principles vetted by experts. The United States Department of Agriculture (n.d.) hosts a page entitled "What You Should Know About Popular Diets" at nutrition.gov. The page has links to more information on each of the following:

- Beware of products promising miracle weight loss
- Know the science: Nine questions to help you make sense of health research

- Know the science: The facts about health news stories
- Choosing safe and successful weight loss programs
- Weighing the claims in diet ads
- Finding the truth: Reliable nutrition and health information

Know That Some Junk Foods Are Designed to Be Addictive

We mentioned the addictive nature of some snack foods in Chapter 3 as the reason Jane only buys crunchy cheese curls for potluck picnics. *New York Times* reporter Michael Moss (2013) spent four years researching the food company strategies that led to those foods we eat mindlessly or continue to eat when we should feel full. They use a concept called sensory-specific satiety. Foods with distinct, full flavors are easy to stop eating—we savor the specific tastes and stop. But foods that don't have a specific flavor punch (think of cheese curls that are part cheese, part salt, part who knows) call on our taste buds to have another and another and so on.

In talking with scientists and researchers at Frito-Lay, Moss learned that they spend up to $30 million a year exploring food qualities such as crunch, aroma, and the feel in your mouth. They have a $40,000 machine that helps pinpoint just the right amount of crunch in chips! Here's a sample of what he learned about what goes into ensuring you can't eat just one:

> To get a better feel for their work, I called on Steven Witherly, a food scientist who wrote a fascinating guide for industry insiders titled, "Why Humans Like Junk Food." I brought him two shopping bags filled with a variety of chips to taste. He zeroed right in on the Cheetos. "This," Witherly said, "is one of the most marvelously constructed foods on the planet, in terms of pure pleasure." He ticked off a dozen attributes of the Cheetos that make the brain say more. But the one he focused on most was the puff's uncanny ability to melt in the mouth. "It's called vanishing caloric density," Witherly said. "If something melts down quickly, your brain thinks that there's no calories in it . . . you can just keep eating it forever."

Yes, the food industry is working against your ability to make healthy choices—unless your why is clear and you're using proven strategies. Look back in Chapter 7 to consider how cognitive steps might help. What might ensure these foods remain treats or are eaten in moderation? Having a few shouldn't leave you vulnerable to the "what the hell" effect. And consider mindfulness, explained next.

One of Jane's colleagues, a school principal, realized that in the midst of a particularly stressful year, she'd settled into some unhealthy habits. While she had no problem exercising before work and packed healthy breakfasts and lunches, that glass of wine before dinner had grown significantly in size. And more often than not, dinner was the kind of comfort food that should be more of a treat than a regular diet. To motivate the elephant, she set a simple goal of no wine and no refined carbs for a month. That gave her time to ask friends for food and recipe recommendations and to "reset" her habits.

Embrace Mindful Eating

How long can you make a cup or glass of your favorite beverage last? Can you turn a bite-sized treat into six bites to better enjoy the textures, detect the different sweet and salty and tangy tastes, and smell the wonderful aromas?

Imagine ordering a plate of just three escargot at a little French café, like you see in Figure 8.1. They'd likely prepare it with three completely different flavor representations in one appetizer as opposed to the usual United States presentation of six snails swimming in garlic butter. Meals in many other countries last *forever* because your hosts assume you wish to savor and enjoy each bite as well as the conversation. This is called mindful eating, and taking the time to actually enjoy what you are eating is one of the healthiest, simplest, cheapest nutrition strategies out there. We found an excellent two-page primer at the United States Department of Veterans Affairs (n.d.) entitled "Mindful Eating," where you'll note that many of the pointers echo some of our core strategies from Chapter 3.

- Listen to your body. Are you hungry, anxious, bored? Identify why you are eating before you take a bite.
- Remember that often the first bite is the most flavorful. Savor it! And the next. Pay attention to all of the senses involved as well as to whether you are still enjoying the flavors. A leader Jane worked with reported that as he tried this with a bag of snack mix, he noticed for the first time that each variety—the peanuts, the pretzels, the cereal bites, the bits of

toasted rye bread—had unique, enjoyable flavors. Before, he'd always downed a handful and thought it all tasted like the rye, which was the strongest flavor. He reported that the novel flavors were so enjoyable that he made the snack-sized bag last over an hour as he was making a long-distance drive.

- Use a timer. Challenge yourself to make a meal last 20 minutes. Challenge yourself to take your last sip of that latte or breakfast tea at the end of a long meeting. If you hate it when beverages go cold (or warm in the summer), invest in a good insulated cup.
- Stop multitasking. Eating while watching television often leads to overeating, as most people miss the signals that they are full.
- Make a one-off choice, or one of those previously decided ways to ensure you're motivating the elephant and shaping the path. For example, commit to one or two routine snack choices to curb hunger that pack both flavor and nutrition. Our current favorites are a handful of nuts, a low-sugar multigrain oat cereal (check labels, as not all are created equal in terms of protein, added sugar, etc.), or a banana.

FIGURE 8.1
Escargot at a French Café

Understand the Influence of Friends on How You Eat

Dr. Nicholas Christakis and Dr. James Fowler (2007), among others, have been researching the effects of friends and family on our food choices and health for decades. In their study they concluded, "Network phenomena appear to be relevant to the biologic and behavioral trait of obesity, and obesity appears to spread through social ties. These findings have implications for clinical and public health interventions" (p. 370). The effect is most pronounced in friends of the same gender. Dr. Traci Mann at the University of Minnesota Health and Eating Lab documented that whether we do or don't grab chocolate chip cookies from the plate in front of us depends on whether our friends do or don't nibble on one (Gwinn, 2019). Read that carefully for the upside: If those around you are good at avoiding temptation, you'll be more likely to avoid it yourself. And the effects seem to last even when you aren't together.

This means having friends who commit to healthy habits can help you keep your commitments. This includes your colleagues!

Watch Out for Scarcity

Be wary of how "I won'ts" such as "I won't eat that food" can backfire. Researchers Sendhil Mullainathan and Eldar Shafir (2013) in their book *Scarcity: Why Having Too Little Means So Much* show that when we don't have enough of something—time, food, friends, money, chocolate—our thoughts often start narrowing, tunneling in on what we don't have. This may be why fad diets that eliminate desired foods seldom work over the long haul.

A Final Thought

As we were finalizing this chapter, the *Washington Post* ran an article titled "Forget About 'Magic Pills': Focus on Sleep, Exercise, Diet, and Cutting Stress" (Aschwanden, 2021). If you're struggling to reclaim your energy, passion, and time, rethinking how you fuel your brain should be a no-brainer.

Blameless Discernment Moment

How we fuel, condition, and rest our bodies is our call. It's important to arm ourselves with solid scientific information and then turn our attention to our own self-management. This is an area where there is a substantial amount of noise. Eat this; don't eat that. Exercise for 30 minutes to get top benefits and so on. This often results in feeling defensive, ashamed, or exasperated, which is not necessarily the intent of the well-meaning individuals who dispense the advice. Remember that blameless discernment is about getting curious about what we are currently doing and what we might want to try changing. It's about paying attention and adjusting. Please don't be discouraged; instead name your why and find your path.

Five Pathways for Individuals to Improve Fueling the Brain

1. **Limits for success.** Remember to limit the changes you try to make at any one time. If you aim for sleep *and* exercise *and* nutrition all at once, you'll use up bandwidth almost as fast in forming new habits as you'll gain it from those new habits! Which habit change is perhaps most urgent and also seems doable? Start there, celebrate success, and then begin on another.

2. **Set routines.** Food routines for breakfast and lunch can be an excellent route for educators seeking good nutrition. The problem with unintentional quick grabs is that many of the choices won't stick with you. Think protein, unrefined carbs, fiber-filled fruits, and vegetables. What works for you?

3. **Find a buddy for your habit change.** Who is working on a similar habit? Establish a time to check in and encourage each other.

4. **Couple something you really enjoy with the new habit you are trying to establish.** Audiobooks and exercise work for us. Other ideas are working out with friends, swapping healthy recipes with colleagues and perhaps sharing samples over lunch, journaling instead of finishing the day with television news, and so on.

5. **Adjust the number of cognitive steps it takes to do something.** Make it more difficult to indulge in ice cream by not keeping it handy or by keeping a bowl of fruit in the kitchen that is already rinsed and ready to grab.

Five Learning Community Leadership Pathways to Support Fueling Everyone's Brains

1. **Consider before sharing.** Is your school's break room a dumping spot for stuff people don't want to eat at home? How many teachers break rooms are a place to bring the extra Halloween candy? Ask yourself if this is something special you really want to share with your coworkers or if it's something you want to unload so you don't feel guilty about throwing it away.

2. **Start a potluck.** Think of how you might plan potlucks for delicious, nutritious gatherings and meetings. As an outside school consultant, Jane loves when schools do this—or find reasonable caterers who will deliver these kinds of options rather than pizza or other processed foods. Taco bars are simple, with meat and vegetarian choices, tortilla or salad bases, and so on. Teachers on a team can sign up for various items for small or large groups. If you aren't familiar with what local restaurants might do beyond box lunches or fried chicken, ask for volunteers to do the research.

3. **Power up meetings.** Build walking and talking into meeting norms whenever possible.

4. **Open school workout facilities to faculty.** Also, create outdoor routes where individuals are encouraged to walk. Because many people like to know how far they have gone, mark the distances or post a map that captures them!

5. **Promote healthy competition.** Some schools have had team contests for walking a certain number of steps. They have given their team a name (e.g., Team Shakespeare in the English department) and have a happy hour prize at the end of contest. Remember to keep it fun, though!

Bandwidth Band Discussion Guide

1. Look back at our opening Aunt Marion story as an example of a character. What character, real or fictional, might best describe your

current self-care routine? Who would you rather be? Draw these two characters and describe them. Share your drawings and encourage each other—what might help you shape the path to get from Character 1 to Character 2?

2. Use the improvisational game "what I like about . . . and" to help each other identify ideas for changing how you fuel your body. One person gives a suggestion. The other person identifies one thing they like about the idea and then adds to it—even if they think it's an impossible suggestion, finding something good in it often sparks new ideas. An exchange might go like this:

Person A: What if you had the same breakfast every school day?

Person B (who loves variety): What I like about that is I could fix them all at once for a week. And let's say it's protein bars. I could mix up flavors.

Person A: What I like about that is you'd save time. And you'd know exactly what nutrition you're getting.

Person B: What I like about that is I'd know the calorie count and have a little more flexibility at lunch.

3. Use the same improvisation technique to come up with a little contest for your group to improve each person's ability to fuel their brain.

9

Staying Connected

From the Bandwidth Survey

_____ I keep my social media use from interfering with what I need to accomplish.

_____ I put my devices away when I'm engaged face to face with friends, family, or colleagues.

_____ I know when I'm absentmindedly resorting to entertainment via my phone and put it down to engage with my surroundings.

_____ My social media habits keep me connected without souring my mood.

_____ When I am driving, I don't text or talk on my phone.

Curiosity Creator

Give your phone to someone else for a couple of hours, an afternoon, an evening, or the afternoon and evening. Take theirs. Agree not to give in to begging. Before settling back to normal with your screen, do some reflection.

- What, if any, emotional responses did you have to not having your phone?
- What activities did you wish you had your phone for?
- What did you do instead of reaching for your phone?
- What was positive about not having your phone?

Modern Connections—and Disconnects

Did you know that scientists are investigating how phones function as digital companions—as something we look to for support, reassurance, camaraderie, and more (Carolus et al., 2019)? Did you know that one of the best models to explain adult usage is to compare phones to pacifiers and other comfort objects (Melumad & Pham, 2020)? None of the researchers deny the benefits of smartphones—in fact, some brought up how using your phone to relieve stress beats reaching for cigarettes or junk food.

However, we hope this image of a phone as a substitute for thumb-sucking gives pause. How do you use your phone? Which habits are beneficial? Which are maladaptive? How does your phone help and hinder nurturing real relationships at work and in your personal life? And how does it affect your bandwidth? Our relationship with the devices we use can interfere with our true priorities (Chapter 5), prompt mindless scrolling without filtering (Chapter 6), scatter our focus (Chapter 7), and even interfere with sleep and physical activity (Chapter 8). Yes, those devices can affect every area of bandwidth.

In her humorous but practical book *How to Break Up with Your Phone: The 30-Day Plan to Take Back Your Life,* Catherine Price (2018) reflects:

> These days, I can't even remember the last time I was bored. Then again, I can't remember a lot of things. Like, for example, the last time my friends and I made it through a meal without anyone pulling out a phone or how it felt to be able to read an entire magazine article in one sitting. Or what I said in the paragraph above this one. Or whose text I was looking at right before I walked into that pole.
>
> Or whatever. My point is, I feel like I can't live without you.
>
> And that's why it's so hard for me to tell you that we need to break up. (p. viii)

We've all probably watched friends stay in rather unproductive relationships with significant others who demand too much attention, complain about any outing where they're not included, or discourage pursuits they used to love. And most of us have stayed in relationships too long, missing signs that things aren't ideal. Let's apply that same kind of thinking to our devices. Is it a healthy relationship? Are new boundaries needed? Your answers play a large role in generating bandwidth.

The depth to which smartphones have permeated society, without our consciously inviting them in, is incredible. While levels of usage seem to have finally stabilized, over 80 percent of Americans are on the web several times a day; a third say they are on constantly (Perrin & Kumar, 2019).

Most people underestimate their screen time; as we mentioned in Chapter 5, if you're curious, newer phones let you track it. Again, though, it's how, not whether, we use our phones that really matters.

The Five Ws of Device Use for Healthy Connections

As you read through the whos, whats, whens, whys, and hows of device usage, take an outside view. Consider how others might view your current phone habits and how they may be fueling or draining your bandwidth bucket.

But before you begin, Figure 9.1 is a little tic-tac-toe of healthy device habits. How many times can your mark three in a row? Do any have you thinking "if only"? Do you wonder why any of these might be good ideas? Read on.

FIGURE 9.1

Tic-Tac-Toe of Healthy Device Habits

I feel happier after seeing what friends have posted on social media.	My phone home screen is free of games or social media that might take me down a mindless path in creativity-dulling ways.	We ask permission before we google something on our phones, even if everyone wants to know the answer.
I have an "I'm driving" message on my phone.	My friends and I have screens-away agreements when we're together.	I have a book on my phone to read so I don't doomscroll or otherwise do stuff I don't want to do.
I've deleted from my phone social media apps that weren't serving me.	I can articulate the purpose of different apps on my phone. I have deliberately chosen to keep them there.	I'm happy snapping group photos and waiting to post them until after our social gathering is over.

Who is your phone keeping you from "seeing"?

> This is one area where I have put strict limits in place. No noti-
> fications, and I check social media once a day for 15 minutes.
> I also do not watch the news. I choose where I will spend my
> media time in ways that will encourage me.
>
> —School Principal

If adults see their phones as comfort objects, other adults view them as competition. Ponder for a moment how phones used to know their place—or, rather, we knew how to keep phones in their place.

You may have seen it in old movies. A server walks up to a table and informs a gentleman (always a man, always a fancy restaurant), "Excuse me, but there's a call for you, sir." Or a mother (always the mother), tethered to a wall phone, covering the mouthpiece while she shouts to a child in another room, "Wait until I've finished this call." Or the teenage daughter at the dinner table, looking longingly toward the kitchen where the phone is ring-ing, knowing she can't excuse herself until the family meal is over, sure her boyfriend is thinking he's being ignored. Oh, the difficulties of days before smartphones. But what about the difficulties of today?

> The visible presence of a smart phone or other digital device during
> a conversation decreases the level of connection people feel with
> each other, and the perceived level of empathy. People conversing
> with casual acquaintances with no cell phone present felt a deeper
> connection than those who had a deeper relationship but had their
> phones on the table. (Misra et al., 2014, p. 31)

We may sometimes make fun of people who insist on phone etiquette, but the above citation illustrates why thinking "anything goes" with devices simply isn't a good idea. Evidence is mounting that the impact goes beyond rudeness. Our brains are wired for human interaction; devices interfere in ways we're only now discovering. Let's look at research we can use to be in the right relationships with phones and with others.

For social relationships in general, researchers have coined the term *techoference* to name device behaviors that interfere with valuable human interactions. A 2015 Pew Research poll (Perrin & Kumar, 2019) showed that

- Close to 90 percent of adults use their devices at social gatherings.
- About 82 percent of the same group said that phone use detracts from real-time conversations.
- Only 25 percent indicated that their own smartphone use lessened the attention they gave to others.

Similar results appear in a study of romantic relationships. Amichai-Hamburger and Etgar (2016) found that partners were clear that multitasking—using phones while supposedly being present with their partner—had a negative effect on their relationships. However, it was their partner's smartphone use, not their own, that was the problem. This pattern of thinking "They're the ones with the problem, not me!" shows up over and over. The root of the problem, though, lies with how our brains have evolved to judge whether someone cares about us by how attentive they are to our needs. Thus, the device becomes competition.

If you have children, you may have noticed that your device usage can affect their behavior. They know they're competing with that phone for your attention. Radesky (2020) found that while cell phones can be handy for distracting children with games, parents overusing devices can result in escalating negative behavior in children. They are quick to interpret, often correctly, that they are being ignored. And negative attention is better than no attention in their little worlds.

In their book *The Big Disconnect: Protecting Childhood and Family Relationships in the Digital Age,* Steiner-Adair and Barker (2013) summarize several studies.

> We also know that babies are often distressed when they look to their parent for a reassuring connection and discover the parent is distracted or uninterested. Studies show that they are especially distressed by a mother's "flat" or emotionless expression, something we might once have associated with a depressive caregiver but which now is eerily similar to the expressionless face we adopt when we stare down to text, stare away as we talk on our phones, or stare into a screen as we go online. (p. 71)

Rationalizations are easy: we're putting out fires at work, we can't ignore texts from friends and family who might really need something, we don't want to insult anyone, and so on. Perhaps it helps to remember that there's a true trade-off in terms of the real-time interactions and the impact on those relationships. In this context, it makes sense to at least take advantage of features such as special ring tones for key individuals.

Learning communities might also look at norms around providing phone numbers to parents for text messages to staff. One school noted that younger teachers readily gave out their numbers but were then dismayed to receive texts at all hours. At a private school, teachers commented that parents pressured them to provide this easy access, commenting that they were paying tuition and deserved this level of connectivity. This is an area where school-wide norms or policies might ensure reasonable parental expectations and less staff guilt or frustration.

In the work context, though, consider the words of Greg McKeown (2014). In his bestseller *Essentialism,* he asks us to rethink our priorities.

> What if we stopped celebrating being busy as a measurement of importance? What if instead we celebrated how much time we had spent listening, pondering, meditating, and enjoying time with the most important people in our lives? (p. 26)

Reflection: For the next 24 hours, when you are with friends or family or colleagues, keep your phone away. And don't bring it out without consciously thinking about whether the people in front of you might be more important than anything in the virtual world.

What is your phone keeping you from doing?

It isn't news that checking emails and looking for "likes" or comments on social media can lead to procrastination. More important, though, these habits that were nonexistent before smartphones may be robbing you of a crucial brain task: daydreaming.

What did you used to do while standing in a line? Waiting for a plane? Idling at a carpool pick-up spot? Watching a show that is far more interesting to your partner than to you? Chances are, you daydreamed. It turns out that this is our brain's default mode when not attending to something specific, and it serves important functions. The brain is still tapping about 95 percent of the energy it uses when engaged in focused thinking. What exactly is it doing? It's accessing recent experiences and interactions, imagining what others are thinking or feeling, and deciding what things mean to us. We come to greater understandings. We make sense of the most unpredictable and irrational things in our lives: other people (Zomorodi, 2017).

Jennifer Odell (2019), in her book *How to Do Nothing*, captures our dire need for leaving ourselves open to daydreaming.

> In times such as these, having recourse to periods of and spaces for "doing nothing" is of utmost importance, because without them we have no way to think, reflect, heal, and sustain ourselves—individually or collectively. There is a kind of nothing that's necessary for, at the end of the day, doing something. When overstimulation has become a fact of life, I suggest that we reimagine #FOMO as #NOMO, the necessity of missing out, or if that bothers you, #NOSMO, the necessity of sometimes missing out. (p. 22)

Reflection: Next time you are standing in line, avoid reaching for your phone. Instead, ponder an upcoming interaction. How might you make it the best it can be?

Why are you reaching for your phone?

> I have definitely noticed that, as my stress level rises, I use social media to disassociate, but I have been more mindful of that as my stress increases to manage the actual stressor in front of me. Tell all the people—it has actually helped!
>
> —Instructional Coach

We need our phones to communicate. They act as extended memory with grocery lists and driving directions. We have endless information at our fingertips, and we can stream shows, play games, read books, follow the news, nostalgically thumb through our photos, check what our friends are doing, and more. But why?

As you reach for your phone, think. "Am I using this to escape boredom or to escape reality? Is it time for the kind of mindless activity that actually increases my bandwidth, and am I choosing wisely? Should I read a book in a focused way? Am I hoping for that dopamine hit that comes from some-one 'liking' my post or responding to my email? Am I using social media to somehow feel better about my life?" Odell again adds a powerful motivation for avoiding this trap: "A simple refusal motivates my argument: refusal to believe that the present time and place, and the people who are here with us, are somehow not enough."

Sifting through our motivations is best done with blameless discernment—and a touch of humility. We've had *many* conversations with people who think they have no issues because they don't have Facebook, Twitter, Instagram, or TikTok on their phones. It's easy to fall into the trap of rationalizing how/why we use our smartphones. "I'm not depressed because of seeing everyone's enhanced-lip photos in Instagram." "I don't waste time looking at pictures of what others ate at restaurants."

Yet people who make these kinds of proclamations may watch endless YouTube videos, play several rounds of *Words with Friends,* doomscroll through news stories, read too many product reviews as they shop for some new gadget, stream PBS documentaries, or complete the day's rounds on their Brainiac or vocabulary-building apps.

Reflection: Look at your home screen. Which apps foster well-being or productivity? Which keep you from being present, from much-needed day-dreaming, or from contentment? Which might you move to the next screen? Which might you delete and only check on a less mobile device?

Now think of your neck, wrist, elbows, and especially your thumbs. Back in 2005, a term was coined for the tendonitis that came with operating a phone keyboard—Blackberry Thumb. What sorts of physical strain do you have from using your phone too often?

How is your phone making you feel?

With our friends and family scattered everywhere, we love how social media allows us to stay connected. Our nieces and nephews keep us updated on their lives, we keep in touch with colleagues so that we can pick up where we left off when we meet in person, and video calls mean we can collaborate easily from anywhere.

However, connecting remotely is *not* a substitute for the face-to-face communication that humans are wired to require. Did you know that composing texts and emails lights up the part of our brain activated by to-do lists? Our brains want to check off these methods of connecting, processing them as tasks instead of communication related to relationships (Steiner-Adair & Barker, 2013). This is partly why it's so tempting to multitask by texting during a meeting or even when driving. We want the satisfaction of completion. This is also why dumb, emotionally charged texts get sent even if we'd hold our tongues in real life. Our brain thinks, "There! Off our plate!" as we fire off a response before calming down. Think of how differently you approach writing a real letter. Or consider how, when talking to someone in person, you adjust what you're saying as you watch their reactions.

Have you heard the term *Zoom fatigue*? Screen time interaction comes with a host of drawbacks that exhaust our brains. According to Dr. Jena Lee (2020), online sessions such as Zoom rob us of much of the nonverbal communication that in actuality makes up a great deal of what is conveyed during in-person communication. We can't see the shifts in body position or feet tapping that enhance what others are saying. Thus, it takes more effort to understand others and respond appropriately.

> Without the help of these unconscious cues on which we have relied since infancy to socioemotionally assess each other and bond, compensatory cognitive and emotional effort is required. In addition, this increased cost competes for people's attention with acutely elevated distractions such as multitasking, the home environment (e.g., family, lack of privacy), and their mirror image on the screen. Simply put, videoconferences can be associated with low reward and high cost.

Turning to social media, we discussed in Chapter 6 the need for filters to keep from being overwhelmed, but there are other drawbacks. For all its benefits, social media doesn't guarantee happiness. If you haven't watched the Netflix film *The Social Dilemma,* created by some of the creators of the biggest social media platforms, carve out 90 minutes to understand the manipulative capabilities, impact on self-esteem, and other disturbing downsides of connecting virtually.

This documentary reveals that social media platforms are not free but in fact come with a heavy price: your attention. Social media platforms need you to be using them in order to collect money from advertisers. Ann gave up social media for the month of October 2020, and within a few short days of halting any Twitter activity, Twitter was after her attention! She received an email: "You've received 14 recent notifications on Twitter! Check them out!"

Many teachers told us that they avoid social media altogether because they have become the targets of angry parents or parents who feel the need to keep them informed on social or even political issues. One school holds weekly staff discussions on social media "wins," difficulties, student issues, and suggested boundaries or strategies that teachers find very useful. Social media seems to be here to stay, and these brief discussions allow for regular updates and support on this fast-changing, ever-present force in our society.

Reflection: We discussed the perils and promise of the artificial intelligence-driven filters these sites provide, but also consider how your emotions can be manipulated.

First, whether it's Facebook or a news site, the filters are designed to give you more of what you've show interest in. Consider the manipulation argument. How are you being manipulated, and how does that affect your brain energy? Do you find yourself more outraged and irritable?

Second, remember that we evolved to seek approval. It's baked into our DNA. How are you affected when people do and don't respond to your social media posts?

When are you using your phone?

Most people seem to have gotten the message that texting and driving is downright reckless. Even hands-free phone calls decrease our field of vision—we stay more focused on the road ahead, decreasing the use of our peripheral vision. This isn't true of conversation with a live passenger or of listening to music or audiotapes. Again, rationalization kicks in to justify our own habits that distract us when we're driving. If you've seen people shaving and driving, applying mascara and driving, reading and driving, or reaching to hand children objects while driving, you've seen this in action.

And driving isn't the only danger zone. Crowley, Madeleine, and Vuillerme (2019) found that using phones while walking, whether to text or to view other apps, causes an irregular gait, with more chances of tripping or slipping. While there isn't evidence of nationwide pedestrian death increases from cell phone use, ER doctors tell of higher injury rates, especially from falls. And remember the tunnel vision effect that phones have; you don't want to become a statistic by stepping into a street without seeing the car or transit vehicle coming your way. Pedestrian deaths were at the highest level since 1988 as we were writing this book (Governors Highway Safety Association, 2020), with driver and pedestrian distraction as contributing factors.

Reflection: Do you make calls while driving? How do you use your phone while walking? Are you falling into the trap of assuming your ability to multitask is above average?

A Final Thought

Jill Andresky, author of *White Collar Sweatshop,* used one worker's comment on emails and cell phones to title a chapter: "They Used to Use a Ball and Chain." Are you sometimes a prisoner of your phone, waiting for a message or afraid of missing out? Remember that up until the introduction of smartphones, these worries didn't exist. How can you make the most of your device without it owning you? Creating this reality is essential to your bandwidth.

Blameless Discernment Moment

Make a T chart. On one side, list your good screen habits. On the other, list your maladaptive screen habits. What do you want to change? Who can you partner with for accountability?

Five Pathways for Individuals to Stay Connected

1. **Phone relationship makeover.** If this chapter has prompted you to go for a total phone relationship makeover, here's how to get started:
   - Use the screen time feature on your smartphone or tablet to determine just how much time you spend using various apps. Then, set a specific goal to better align your screen time with your priorities. What do you want to do less of?
   - Decide what you want to do more of. If you replace a low-value activity with one of higher value to you, you'll use less brain energy than if you merely try to resist an activity. Screen time habits have

characteristics in common with addiction. UCLA's Suzette Glasner-Edwards (2015) recommends finding at least one enjoyable and pleasurable activity that you can pursue instead. The key is to connect with something that you know you will enjoy. Glasner-Edwards suggests predicting on a scale of 1–10 how much you will enjoy the new activity. Then rate it afterward. She finds that people tend to enjoy an activity more than they think they will, so it's important to make that connection.

- Make it easy. Remember that the rider, your brain, knows what you should do. Steering that elephant of habit, though, is tough. The smoother you can make the path, the better. You might delete an offending app, as mentioned above. Or your phone might go in a drawer for a few hours after work or after dinner. Or you might preschedule video coffee chats or online game evenings with friends throughout the month so that they're set to go.
- Reflect weekly on your screen time data. Are you staying true to your goal? Are you ready to set another? Is your phone now a good friend or still one that leads you astray?

2. **Phone-free in nature.** Go outside without a phone and notice the details. Or, put it in airplane mode and look for a detail to photograph. Think you don't have access to nature? Even simple weeds, like in Figure 9.2, grow around city trees, sidewalk cracks, and more. To what do you give your attention?

3. **Invite feedback.** If your work requires online activity after hours, are you aware of how those who are important to you view those work habits? Gather feedback from them. Negotiate solutions together. Would they rather you finish up everything the minute you get home to be available the rest of the evening? Are they willing to handle more mealtime prep and clean-up so that you have more time with them? And, with blameless discernment, consider whether you are being as efficient as possible or if you need to review tips for focusing and being more efficient from Chapter 7.

4. **Talk with strangers.** Isn't it funny how quickly you realize you've left your phone at home? Have you formed a habit to check for your phone before you leave? Have you reached for it and discovered it

FIGURE 9.2
Simple Weeds

wasn't there? Do you wonder what you will you do instead of mind-lessly scrolling when waiting or stressed or bored? Remember that we are wired to connect with people, even strangers, as it is part of our ancestral DNA. When was the last time you struck up a conversation while waiting in a coffee line? A colleague of ours met her husband on the London Tube. What are the chances of that happening today?

5. **Prioritize real calls.** Remember that real phone calls, whether or not they include video feed, are better than texts for relationship health. While few of us enjoy overhearing personal conversations, consider having a list of who you might contact if you're in a spot conducive to making a call and have some downtime. Jane calls an elderly aunt who lives in another city and struggles with other forms of technology. Do you have friends who'd love to chat if you texted, "Is now a good time?" When might this be a better alternative than scrolling through social media or playing games?

Five Learning Community Leadership Pathways to Support Staying Connected

1. **Norm "away" messages all day.** "Not available" email messages have to start from the top. Set up an auto reply that says, "I generally check emails at set times during the day and will get back to you soon. If you need to speak to someone immediately, please. . . ." Leaders who have tried this find that almost no one uses the immediate contact information, and this strategy keeps you from being diverted from the people in front of you.

   Learning communities have adopted the following potential norms:
   - Do not answer emails between 5:00 p.m. and 8:00 a.m. While some people may choose to write some during these hours, they can be scheduled without being sent.
   - Put cell phones away in meetings. Ring alerts should be for family members only.
   - Reduce use of "reply all" by encouraging thinking before clicking or using bcc instead of cc so that replies go only to the sender.
   - No Friday afternoon meetings and no Monday morning meetings.

2. **Phoneless driving.** At every opportunity, discourage driving and conversing. We've found that educators in rural locations may still see this as a good use of time if they have long commutes on country roads. It is still dangerous!

3. **Create a culture of connecting and make it fun.** Keep a deck of "We're Not Really Strangers" cards in the teachers' lounge to spur conversation. The questions are as simple as "Do I look like a cat or a dog person?" or "Is there anyone who has changed your life but doesn't know it?"

4. **Take a collective social break.** Make this time as important as the topic at hand. Who did you talk to this week? What did you learn about that colleague? Remember outcomes and relationships. Visit the teachers' lounge and see people in person. People who know each other personally work better together.

5. **Go old school instead of using devices.** We rely on our phones for nearly everything we do. What can be accomplished without screens?

Bandwidth Band Discussion Guide

1. Is your phone your friend or your foe? How do you know?
2. Describe your current social media habits. How do you feel when you are using social media? How does it affect your energy? How about your opinion of yourself or others?
3. If you could alter time and circumstances where cell phone use, and all of its bells and whistles, could be just right, what would that look like? What might be different in your personal life or in your learning community? Moving forward, how can you use these ideas to inform your behavior?

10

Making Time Work for You

From the Bandwidth Survey

_____ I manage multiple deadlines (i.e., no sudden realizations that I have overlooked something).

_____ I build my schedule to allow for meeting overruns and traffic delays.

_____ I am aware of the distracting dangers of email notifications, phone calls, and more, and I remove from my immediate environment those that interrupt my concentration.

_____ I have strategies to delay important decisions until I can give them my full attention, especially at the end of long meetings or tiring days.

Curiosity Creator

What are your reactions to the following quotes?

- "Which is easier: trying to find time or trying to make time?" —Kise and Holm
- "Time is a created thing. To say 'I don't have time' is to say 'I don't want to.'" —Lao Tsu
- "All we have to decide is what to do with the time that is given to us." —J. R. R. Tolkien, *The Fellowship of the Ring*
- "It is the time you have wasted for your rose that makes your rose so important." —Antoine de Saint-Exupéry, *The Little Prince*

- "You can have it all. Just not all at once." —Oprah Winfrey
- "Time is a game played beautifully by children." —Heraclitus, *Fragments*

Making Friends with the Precious Gift of Time

As you look through the survey questions related to making time work for you, it's difficult not to have thoughts like the following:

- Managing multiple deadlines? I could do that if I had some say in the first place over what needs to be done around here!
- Building my schedule for overruns and delays? Those school bells keep ringing no matter what students need!
- Distracting dangers of notifications? What about loudspeaker announcements, knocks on my door from students who really need help, safety drills, and so on?
- Delaying important decisions? It seems like everything needs to be decided yesterday!

We hear you. And we don't want to lose sight of the many pressures on educator time (see Figure 10.1).

We get tired. Our minds wander. We need food, sleep, and physical activity. Once we understand that just pushing through isn't the answer to finding more time, we can instead use helpful strategies to make the most of the time we have.

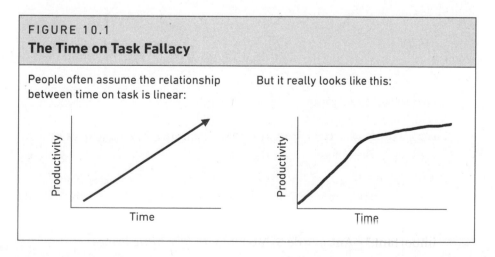

FIGURE 10.1
The Time on Task Fallacy

People often assume the relationship between time on task is linear:

But it really looks like this:

Let's look again at apeirogon thinking about bandwidth and all the facets of your individual responsibilities and your learning community's responsibilities. Remember that the whole point of the bandwidth survey is

- To identify where you can improve your bandwidth;
- To increase your energy; and
- To effectively engage in the great mission of helping all children succeed while honoring your own priorities.

Even if you can't control everything, you can reclaim your energy, passion, and time by focusing on what you *can* change.

This isn't as simple a platitude as "you can always choose your attitude" but a much deeper truth. In the big picture of life, you are choosing your priorities. And, as more people in your learning community come to the realization that prioritizing everything means nothing is actually a priority, and as they collectively pull together to accomplish audacious yet realistic goals, time might begin to work for everyone. Let's start with the true meaning of priorities and then move on to specific ways you can make time.

Claim Your Priority

If you search for articles on priorities, you will see verbs such as *ordering, setting, managing, identifying, listing, ranking,* and so on. Jane, the grammar geek, did a quick perusal of the 12 different tenses of English verbs and realized these are used for continuous tenses:

- Present continuous: I am setting priorities.
- Present perfect continuous: I have been setting priorities.
- Past continuous: I was setting priorities.
- Past perfect continuous: I have been setting priorities.

These articles are all written as if you're *continuously* adjusting and fiddling with priorities. These aren't the kinds of priorities we're talking about. We're talking about rock-solid, foundational principles around which you organize your work and your life rather than a to-do list or a strategic plan. Thus, we didn't title this section "Order Your Priorities" or "Manage Your Priorities" but instead are asking you to claim them!

In his book *Essentialism,* Greg McKeown (2014) points out:

The word priority came into the English language in the 1400s. It was singular. It meant the very first or prior thing. It stayed singular for the next five hundred years. Only in the 1900s did we pluralize the term and start talking about priorities. Illogically, we reasoned that by changing the word we could bend reality. Somehow we would now be able to have multiple "first" things. . . . But when we try to do it all and have it all, we find ourselves making trade-offs at the margins that we would never take on as our intentional strategy. When we don't purposefully and deliberately choose where to focus our energies and time, other people—our bosses, our colleagues, our clients, and even our families—will choose for us, and before long we'll have lost sight of everything that is meaningful and important. We can either make our choices deliberately or allow other people's agendas to control our lives. (pp. 15–16)

Can you see the difference?

You've probably heard some version of a demonstration where the speaker places several large rocks in a jar, filling it to the top, and then asking, "Can I fit in any more?" After his audience answers, "No," he proceeds to pour in first pebbles, which fill in spaces all the way to the bottom, then sand, then water. He then asks, "What is my point?" When someone replies, "You can always make room for more," he corrects, "No, you have to put in the rocks first or they won't fit." *That's* the kinds of priorities we're talking about. Identify them and you can make your time work for you.

We've talked in other chapters about where our time seems to go in this more automated yet busier age, but let's look a little deeper at how you can ensure your major priorities or values—student well-being, self-care, relationships, excellence in the areas you've chosen to influence, and so on—stay your priorities.

Know Your Organizing Style

One key to this kind of priority focus is being aware of your own organizing style. Again, with blameless discernment, think about which of the following best describes how you approach what order you'll do things. Are you . . .

- First in, first out? Do you keep a running to-do list, adding to the bottom, usually working on items in order while crossing them off from top to bottom?
- Inspiration-driven? Do you tend to do first what you have the most energy for?
- Urgency-driven? Do you tend to tackle first what others are asking you to do?
- Project-driven? Do you identify what needs to be done now on each project to keep it on track for the final deadline and organize that way?

All of these approaches have their merits for certain environments, responsibilities, and goals. However, they all have drawbacks. Knowing which is your strength—and default—can help you become more mindful of not overusing it. Think about these related traps, blind spots, and remedies.

If you tend to be first in, first out, you may suddenly realize that something further down your list needed attention a while ago. You may not be missing deadlines, but you may find yourself scrambling to meet them, perhaps losing concentration or flow as you strive to meet your obligations. Try making a more flexible to-do list. Write each item on sticky notes that can be moved around, or create an electronic document that makes it easy to reorder the items.

If inspiration-driven describes you best, some things might be ignored until you're looking at a pile of things you don't really want to do and struggling to find motivation. See what happens if you move to a desired task as a reward for completing something you typically avoid.

Urgency-driven educators are often stuck in the dilemma of trying to please everyone and losing track of their own priorities. They may end up feeling like martyrs or failures, as you simply can't please everyone, nor does ignoring your own priorities work for you or for your learning community in the long run. Practice gaging whether what you are being asked to do is as important as what you were planning to do. If the phrase "your lack of planning isn't my emergency" rings true, have you created expectations that you'll clean up everyone else's messes?

If you're more in the project-driven category, you may stay on track toward your goals, but you might also miss some in-the-moment opportunities, fail to entertain new ideas or rethink your approach, or gloss over what others see as most important. How can you plan for flexibility when it's beneficial?

Whatever your style, doing a double take on what you ask yourself or others to do is a good idea. One helpful method is to think through why you're doing this work and whether you should be doing this work. Think of a few tasks you engaged with yesterday, during the past week, or on your current to-do list. Use the flow chart in Figure 10.2 to consider whether they are productive, bandwidth-building, and worthwhile, or if they are unproductive, draining, or distracting.

Now rethink what you plan to do today—and this week. What might you do to ensure your work will reflect your true priorities—and those of your learning community?

One middle school accidentally created unnecessary work with what seemed like a helpful policy of requiring teachers to make midterm phone

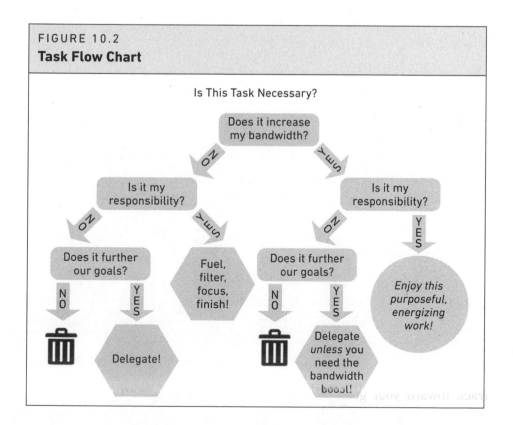

FIGURE 10.2
Task Flow Chart

calls to parents or guardians if a student's grades weren't acceptable. When a specialist with 300 students was reprimanded for not completing the calls, he produced his log showing that over a third of the 100 phone numbers he was given were disconnected. Of those he reached, many complained that they'd received multiple "bad news" calls. The leaders who had implemented the policies apologized for not getting input first from those who would be doing the work.

One grade-level team had an honest discussion about their organizing styles and realized that three shared inspiration-driven traits while the fourth identified with project-driven. She commented, "I *know* how much is on my plate. When I say I can or can't do something, I really know whether I can and will follow through. I feel like the rest of you say yes in a moment of inspiration and then don't realize things are falling off your plates." The others agreed and decided to use the plate analogy more actively as they discussed team responsibilities and deadlines.

Beware the Tunnel Effect

Besides your own natural work style, your perceptions of the pressures you are under can affect your ability to make time work for you. If you feel that you simply don't have enough time, the consequences of a scarcity mindset may come into play.

We mentioned in Chapter 8 that scarcity is having less than you think you need (Mullainathan & Shafir, 2013). Whether it's scarcity of time, relationships, money, professional growth opportunities, water, food, or just about anything important to us, not having enough causes us to think and think and think about what we don't have. Worse, we can end up with "tunnel vision," where scarcity causes us to ignore other things that we need to focus on. The tunneling effect keeps you from seeing other important goals or needs. Think of how lack of food, money, autonomy, or a sense of belonging can drive unwise behaviors. This is partly because tunneling takes away perspective and we lose sight of other priorities.

If your situation includes scarcity in a critical area in your life, please take the perspective of blameless discernment. For example, some teachers are underpaid and struggle to put food on the table; this is still a data point that affects overall bandwidth. Remember that bandwidth is based on brain science and can't be increased by willpower alone, and it is essential to balance work priorities and home priorities. Ask yourself, is it time to look to outside resources or to trusted people who might have new ideas that you can't see on your own due to the tunnel effect?

Scarcity of time is often debilitating because of this tunnel effect. Imagine how the brain gets hijacked by the overarching, pounding thought "I don't have enough time!" Down goes bandwidth, and down go efficiency and effectiveness. You deal with pressing needs, which inhibits thinking about other goals. In sum, thinking you don't have enough time robs you of even more time.

Being realistic about what can be accomplished is key to avoiding the effects of time scarcity. One of the best ways to do this is to assume you won't have enough time. A better way to think of this is to use the concept of "slack." Assume you'll need an extra 10 minutes in the morning to get out the door. Assume you need to allow a good 10 minutes in between scheduled meetings with parents or students. Assume that this year's group of students will need a full day more than last year's group to master a key learning target. Assume that grading papers will take longer than your first estimate. Be realistic about what you can accomplish. Account for possible delays and avoid cutting things too close.

What happens if you don't need the slack you've built into your schedule? You can always put it toward relationships, recreation, rest, or any of the other "big rocks" in your priorities that seem so difficult to fit in. What you *don't* want to do, of course, is arrive early at a meeting only to use those 10 minutes to mindlessly scroll on your device when you could be getting to know someone, reading a book, engaging in meditation, or otherwise fueling your brain.

Aim for Distraction-Free

Another key to making your time work for you is to eliminate as many distractions as possible. We discussed the addictive nature of notifications from device apps in Chapter 9. Remember that, even if you don't take the next step of reading a text or email after hearing that signal from your phone, you'll use up bandwidth trying to ignore it. And if you do check it, it can take up to 20 minutes to get back to your original level of concentration. That is a lot of your precious time gone forever. How inconvenient should checking your phone be? As inconvenient as it takes to remove temptation when your priority is concentration.

Beyond turning off notifications, make sure those around you understand—for your sake and for theirs—that interruptions extend the time a task will take far longer than the actual interruption. Maybe what they wish to ask of you will only take 5 minutes, but it might add another 15 minutes to an hour-long task as you struggle to pick up where you left off. This information helped us negotiate with our families with comments such as "I'll be ready to help with dinner in an hour if I can work uninterrupted. It'll be more like 90 minutes if I can't have that hour."

Background noise is another distraction, but it can also be beneficial. Being smart about how you use it is another key to making time work for you. A paper by Mehta, Rui, and Cheerma (2012) demonstrated that "a moderate level of ambient noise (70db) enhances performance on creative tasks" (p. 784). That's the general level of noise in a coffee shop! Have you ever noticed how well you can concentrate at a Starbucks? At home or school, try setting up background noise to work in your favor; Jane writes best with familiar modern bluegrass playlists running in the background (e.g., Nickel Creek and Psychograss). She doesn't even notice the words or when her toe is tapping. Others benefit from white noise.

When might background noise be a distraction? Maybe an intriguing hallway conversation or argument stands in the way of your efficiency. Or perhaps you hear a pick-up basketball game you'd love to join. If you find yourself straining to fill in the details of a distant conversation or notice your mind drifting to something you'd rather be doing, then you are distracted. Take some time to ensure background noise is a help and not a hinderance.

Slowing Down Decisions

Another factor in using time well is the *when* of decisions. Think about when your learning community or your team tackles major decisions. Is it often during after-school meetings when everyone is tired? Have you ever felt or heard a current in the room such as "Let's just get this over with" rather than the purposeful deliberation an issue might warrant?

One of the best ways to avoid decision fatigue, discussed in Chapter 6, is to delay decisions until morning. If you've spent an entire day grading papers, stack them in order of excellence at the end of the day and assign final points in the morning. If you've conducted several job interviews, delay the final hiring decision until morning. If you're writing a difficult communication email, leave it as a draft until your brain is fresh in the morning.

In *The Intelligence Trap,* David Robson (2019) suggests that to make the best decisions, write down your first gut choice and then come back to reflect on it. How might you not be right? What kinds of bias might come into play? Who might know something you don't know? Even if you come to the same conclusion, you'll have tackled it at a fresher moment. We think of a school board who interviewed superintendent candidates all day and made the hiring decision that night. It may have been the right decision, but would anyone have questioned an overnight delay? No, and there'd have been little chance of decision fatigue.

Delegation can also help. What decisions can be made by others? Even though they might make a few mistakes at first, what might you allow others to decide? There's a fine line between ensuring that everything is done well and trying to control things you don't need to control—or shouldn't control.

A Final Thought

Making time work for you comes down to priorities. If making the right decision is more important than making a decision right now, you'll sleep on it. If finding uninterrupted blocks of time is important, you'll get rid of distractions. If being dependable is important, you'll build in slack and improve how you handle your to-do list.

If this seems to border on the impossible, given the demands on your time, try a few experiments. What happens to your bandwidth if you leave earlier than you think is necessary to drive somewhere? What if you block off that 60 minutes to concentrate? What other small steps come to mind as you go through the individual pathways suggested below? Give time a chance to work for you, not against you.

Blameless Discernment Moment

Reflect on your organization style. Are you more first in, first out, inspiration-driven, urgency-driven, or project-driven? When and how has this style been an asset or a liability? What specifically have you noticed about times that this style brought less than optimal results? What might you do differently next time?

Five Individual Pathways for Making Time Work for You

1. **Stop being available.** Remember from Chapter 7 the addictive nature of emails, texts, and phone calls. Again, challenge the mindset of needing to be constantly available by expanding the time between "checks." Experiment to find the optimal balance between availability and uninterrupted focus.

2. **Place your goals in plain sight.** Know your overall goals, commitments, and objectives. Display them where you can easily be reminded of them. When in scarcity mode, you aren't likely to go searching for these items mentally or physically. Therefore, keep them visible.

3. **Choose your focus.** In his book *Hyperfocus: How to Work Less and Achieve More,* Chris Bailey (2018) asks you to consider how often during the day you *choose* how to focus your attention. Here are examples of how choosing can enhance how time works for you.

   • Do you complete tasks or emails as they come up, or do you prioritize them?

   • Do you build slack into your schedule by, for example, checking the commute time before getting in the car?

   • Do you silence your phone when you need to concentrate?

   • Do you manage your environment to minimize distractions and maximize focus and engagement? Note that sometimes too little stimulation can be a distraction, causing your brain to wander!

   • Do you brainstorm or network to find more efficient ways to get necessary work done (unattractive but productive)?

In other words, unless you deliberately choose, others will choose for you, syphoning off your bandwidth!

4. **Individualize your time.** Do you arrange your schedule around when you are most productive? Even if you don't have control over when your prep periods are, you do have control over what you do during those periods. Early birds might tackle the deeper tasks earlier in the day, saving the email correspondence for later. Night owls might do the opposite. How might you swap responsibilities or otherwise change your schedule, at work or home, to take advantage of your most productive moments?

5. **Choose three.** Decide on three priorities for the day. Bailey (2018) suggests identifying the three by considering what is most urgent and what is most consequential. Get specific and you're three times as likely to accomplish those things (Gollwitzer & Brandstätter, 1997) *if,* of course, you can realistically estimate how long each will take.

Five Learning Community Leadership Pathways to Support Making Time Work

1. **Build in slack!** If meetings are before school, give teachers slack to get to their rooms. During the day? Give them more than passing time. After school? We've never seen teachers upset if a meeting ends early.

2. **Reinstate "do not disturb" signs and spaces.** Have everyone get creative with door signs indicating they're in the midst of one of those crucial 60-minute periods of brain concentration. "Deep Thought Zone." "Focus Hour Happening—Please Wait." What can you come up with? And, if teachers share office space or otherwise lack places amenable to deep concentration, how can you create them?

3. **Create an email policy.** Ensuring that everyone benefits from only occasionally checking emails requires a policy and modeling from the top, and staff need to know that everyone is following it. They can then feel confident in communicating this information to parents and others so there are realistic expectations about response times.

4. **Delay decisions.** Create a norm of noting whether an upcoming decision is weighty enough to deserve wait time, whether individuals or leadership or teams are making the call. Questions such as "Do we need to sleep on this?" or "Does this deserve percolation time?" can ensure that the tone of an email is correct, that disciplining a student manages to be fair and equitable, or that a school policy or hiring decision is the best it can be and not clouded by our tendency to crave closure at the end of a long day.

5. **Think vision and reality.** One way to guard against creating a scarcity mentality, where teachers are distracted by worries over not having enough time to carry out everything required by school initiatives, is to ensure your plans are realistic. If you're a big-picture thinker, who might help you chart out whether your learning community actually has the time, professional development resources, finances, and other resources to follow through on the plan? When visions aren't realistic, leaders may think they are setting high standards for progress by pushing audacious goals, but in reality they frequently have lost track of what is actually being prioritized. As the reality of scarcity sets in, things are randomly falling off people's plates.

Bandwidth Band Discussion Guide

1. Compare your distraction level today to what it was a year ago, 5 years ago, and 10 years ago. What has changed?

2. How has the ability to build slack in your schedule changed in that same period? What accounts for some of the differences?

3. How have group dynamics in education changed, and how do these changes affect distractions and capacities to stay on top of schedules and make time work for you? What changes are you contemplating for yourself and your learning community?

11

Using the Bandwidth Survey with Your Learning Community

Curiosity Creator

What have you heard or read about the length of time it takes to form a new habit or get used to a "new normal"?

A. 21 days

B. 30 days

C. 60 days

D. Six months

Perhaps you've heard the 21- to 30-day time period as a fact. It's based on ideas in the bestselling book *Psycho-Cybernetics* by Maxwell Maltz (1960). He noted that it took his plastic surgeon patients about 21 days to get used to the look of a new nose or for an amputee's "phantom limb" sensation to fade. Considering other such changes, he wrote that it takes a minimum of 21 days for such mental images to change—and that got extrapolated to the "21 days to change a habit" mantra. Or 30 days.

However, research involving subjects trying to form a variety of new habits paints a different picture. On average, it takes 66 days, with individuals falling in a range from 18 to 254 days, depending on the habit. In an article titled "How Long Does It Actually Take to Form a New Habit? (Backed by Science)," James Clear (2014) points out three reasons why this research should encourage us:

1. You can stop judging yourself if it takes you months to change a habit.
2. The research showed that lapses are normal and don't keep people from changing the habit.
3. We can stop looking at forming habits as an event and treat it as a process.

As you delve into the process of improving bandwidth in your learning community, recognize that this journey may take a few months. If you're committed to the goal, little setbacks won't derail your overall progress. And perhaps most important, if it's a journey, you might as well have fun along the way.

In this chapter, we'll look at how to find the best steps for your learning community's unique journey to better bandwidth *and* provide some ways to make it fun.

A Learning Community Mindset for Exploring Bandwidth Results

Think of administering the Brain Energy and Bandwidth Survey to your staff as similar to a wellness visit to your doctor. Simple yet effective measurements (e.g., temperature, blood pressure, cholesterol) provide insights into your health and can pinpoint what might need more attention.

Similarly, being able to look at aggregated data through the bandwidth survey can answer a few crucial questions:

1. Do learning community members believe they are energized, effective, efficient, and engaged?
2. Are any groups—teachers, administrators, specialists, and so on—more at risk of having inadequate bandwidth than others? Note that these first two questions help you assess the level of bandwidth in your learning community.
3. Do learning community members believe that learning community norms and policies support their individual bandwidth? This question helps you think about questions like "How did we get to where we are? Is this where we want to be?" Remember, the number one predictor of individual bandwidth scores is whether they believe organizational norms and policies support good bandwidth.

4. Do the levels of individual bandwidth indicate that their sense of self-efficacy and engagement are sustainable? This question takes a long view even if staff is still motivated and engaged so that you can shape a better environment for your ongoing mission.

Self-Care: One Component of Bandwidth

Perhaps one of the gifts of the COVID-19 pandemic was a heightened awareness of the crucial need for educators to engage in self-care if they are to bring their best selves to students and stay in this highly stressful profession for the long haul. However, self-care is only one of the components of overall bandwidth, covered mostly in Chapter 8. Via the aggregated data, you can check whether your learning community might benefit from paying more attention to the other areas, such as focusing attention (Chapter 7), balancing priorities (Chapter 5), and so on.

If only the concept of self-care is emphasized, a community runs the risk of placing the burden for adequate bandwidth on individuals while ignoring how the organization does or doesn't support all six components our research identified. To ensure that you take a balanced approach with blameless discernment, we suggest gathering a team of interested stakeholders representing leadership, teachers, support staff, and others to examine the data using the ideas in this chapter. We suggest that you keep two huge ideas in mind: how organizational norms and policies affect individual bandwidth and the impact of adult bandwidth on student social and emotional learning.

Do Our Norms and Policies Support Good Bandwidth for Individuals?

Remember this figure from Chapter 4 (Figure 11.1)? People can't do it alone.

Providing the survey to your whole staff allows for a data-informed discussion of whether people have the bandwidth to be energized, effective, efficient, and engaged.

Think about that. If we want educators to be energized, effective, efficient, and engaged, let's stop saying, "This is the way things are," and start finding ways to ensure they have the bandwidth they need. We hope this chapter helps you get creative.

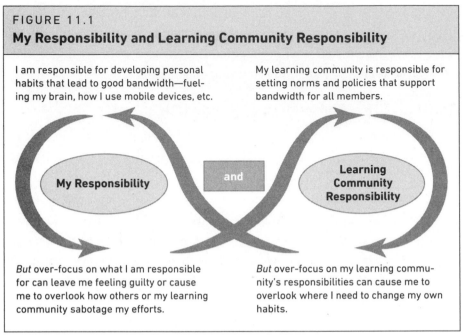

FIGURE 11.1

My Responsibility and Learning Community Responsibility

I am responsible for developing personal habits that lead to good bandwidth—fueling my brain, how I use mobile devices, etc.

My learning community is responsible for setting norms and policies that support bandwidth for all members.

My Responsibility

and

Learning Community Responsibility

But over-focus on what I am responsible for can leave me feeling guilty or cause me to overlook how others or my learning community sabotage my efforts.

But over-focus on my learning community's responsibilities can cause me to overlook where I need to change my own habits.

Source: Adapted from Johnson (2020).

Do Adults Have Enough Bandwidth to Model Emotional Intelligence?

During the COVID-19 pandemic, much was written on how to pay attention to the social and emotional needs of staff as well as students. For us, this only highlighted how little we pay attention to the developmental needs of educators. What do we mean?

For years, we've worked with leaders in organizations big and small to improve their emotional intelligence (EQ). Consider Figure 11.2—what has become known as SEL is another name for the EQ model developed decades ago by Reuven Bar-On.

The EQ model combines social awareness and relationship skills into the interpersonal category and adds stress management. Think about that in the context of bandwidth.

- Those who researched adult EQ found that the ability to manage emotions appropriately under stress is a crucial component of overall emotional intelligence.

FIGURE 11.2	
SEL and the EQ Model	
Components of SEL	**Components of EQ**
Self-awareness	Self-perception
Self-management	Self-expression
Social awareness	Interpersonal
Relationship skills	Decision making
Responsible decision making	Stress management

Sources: SEL model (Collaborative for Academic, Social and Emotional Learning, 2021). EQi 2.0 model (Multi-Health Systems, 2011).

- Your bandwidth affects your overall ability to apply your emotional intelligence.
- If you use up your bandwidth on critical-thinking tasks, on applying willpower to not eat that doughnut, or on being patient with students— or if you fail to effectively fuel your brain via diet, sleep, and exercise— you have less bandwidth available to modulate your emotions.

In other words, no one "arrives" at the point where they are emotionally intelligent. There are all kinds of ways to improve emotional self-awareness, expression, and so on to increase the size of your bandwidth fuel tank, just as we can use SEL to increase the same in students. But if adult bandwidth is low, how can we model emotional intelligence to students?

Emotional Intelligence, Bandwidth, and Student Discipline

Let's look at the impact of EQ and bandwidth on just one area in schools: the ability to calmly and equitably discipline students when their behavior isn't acceptable. We've been conducting a poll of convenience, asking school leaders we interact with, "When teachers discipline students, what percentage of the time do you think they do so while hijacked by negative emotions?" Their answers: 80–90 percent of the time.

We ask it this way because those negative emotions usually indicate we're still being ruled by our reactionary habits—our decisions are likely to be colored by bias as well as the frustration, fear, anger, or other emotions tied up in our judgment of ourselves, students, the administrators, or circumstances (see Chapter 1 for a deeper discussion of these ways of judging).

It is really hard to employ empathy, explore alternatives, consider both equity and consistency, and stay calm when one is hijacked by emotions. *And* the lower one's bandwidth, the easier it is to get hijacked.

Placing this dilemma—expecting students to grow via SEL while not attending to adult EQ—within the context of your bandwidth discussions allows for blameless discernment. Instead of "Why can't you discipline in a level-headed way?" the conversation turns to "How do we increase our bandwidth so we have enough available when, inevitably, student behaviors trigger us?"

Interpreting Your Results

To examine your data with blameless discernment, it is often helpful to look at the "Individual Outcomes" section first. This gives a snapshot of whether people feel energized, effective, efficient, and engaged! You might interpret your results as you would a traffic light. If the average score is above 3.5, you've got a green light—members of the learning community are all rowing in the same, good direction, and they're rowing fast.

If average scores are between 2.5 and 3.5, take a harder look at the data. Where are you seeing some "yellow lights" that might need attention? And if scores are below 2.5, where are the flashing red lights that indicate your staff is in danger of being deenergized, inefficient, ineffective, and disengaged? That should sound scary.

Then, turn to the overall total bandwidth scores. What is the average for your whole professional learning community? Make sure to look at the disaggregated data as well to locate any patterns in which groups of employees might be experiencing undue stress.

Compare those scores with the descriptions below of visible behaviors and attitudes in learning communities within each bandwidth score range.

Behaviors Associated with Good Bandwidth (range 90–120)

- Humor and optimism are hallmarks of conversations about learning.
- High self-efficacy results in collective focus; work is accomplished in a reasonable amount of time.

- Adults are able to discipline students from a place of calm, balancing empathy, equity, and consistency.
- Teachers enjoy collaborative meeting time, benefitting both from improved teaching skills and supportive relationships.
- Learning community members are satisfied with how they are balancing work life and personal life.

Behaviors Associated with Mediocre Bandwidth (range 60–90)

- Self-efficacy and engagement scores may still be high, but learning community members are concerned about balancing work life and personal life.
- Collective efficacy and focus are present, but staff increasingly expresses concerns regarding issues such as competing school strategic priorities or increased needs of their students.
- More reactionary incidents occur as educators engage in student discipline.
- Absenteeism or other indicators of decreases in well-being may be on the rise.
- There are more complaints about meetings and more multitasking behaviors as people struggle to fit in everything.
- People are losing patience with people, things, processes, or circumstances in one or more areas of their lives.

Behaviors Associated with Problematic Bandwidth (range below 60)

- The learning community is operating from a "mission critical" stance most of the time.
- Instead of collective efficacy, there is a feeling of learned helplessness in meetings—staff believe that no matter their effort, the needs of students will overwhelm their capacity.
- There is lack of camaraderie, impatience with others, or avoidance behaviors, as socializing is seen as wasted time.
- Burnout and disengagement are evident; some may fantasize about quitting their current roles.
- People are staying up far too late binge-watching television or engaging in other mindless activities to claim "me time."

No matter your aggregate scores, what is the overall "feel" in your community? While bandwidth can't solve everything, it *can* ensure that you're fixing things that can be fixed so that people have as much capacity as possible for both work and life.

But What If Teacher Efficacy and Engagement Are Still High?

If your learning community's scores for the following individual outcome questions are high, but bandwidth averages are mediocre or low, congratulations! For now. Unfortunately, the neuroscience we relied on to build the bandwidth survey suggests that this is not a sustainable state of affairs. If bandwidth is mediocre or low, how long will people be able to continue to score high on these items?

- Your overall sense of energy
- Your engagement level at work
- Your sense of self-efficacy—your ability to complete tasks and reach goals
- Your ability to concentrate and get things done efficiently and effectively
- Your ability to balance work life and personal life
- Your sense of meaning and purpose derived from your work responsibilities

Low individual bandwidth and high scores on energy, engagement, and efficacy can also mean that people are directing the majority of their energy toward work. This could have consequences in their personal life. Overfocusing on one area of the interdependent priorities of work and personal life (see Chapter 5) eventually brings unintended consequences in both areas.

It may also be that your learning community is unaware of the real impact of low bandwidth on performance because everyone has grown used to operating in crisis mode. Have you ever gotten a good night's sleep and realized you didn't even know you were that tired? We can muscle through low bandwidth because we are "so used to it," but on the other end can be the following outcomes:

- Student discipline impatience
- Staff conflict

- Sour mood contagion
- People staying too late
- Burnout and the high rate of teachers leaving the profession

Let's move on to what to do with the data and how to create an actionable, doable, impactful plan for increasing collective bandwidth.

Identifying Action Steps

Every organization we've worked with has found some bandwidth areas in need of attention. As you read through, consider the following:

- What is the low-hanging fruit? Doing something quickly may be more important than immediately tackling the lowest-scoring item if the latter is complex.
- How many changes can you handle well?
- How can you avoid overpromising?

You're looking for three or four areas to concentrate on so as not to overwhelm or overpromise. If you get those implemented, go for another. Don't add sweeping initiatives on top of all your others.

That said, one organization we worked with quickly identified 10 easy-to-implement, high-impact changes. When they were announced, staff applauded. What were they? No emails from 5:00 p.m. to 8:00 a.m. No meetings on Mondays before 10:00 and on Fridays after 2:00 to better handle workflow for the week. They added an asynchronous training on email efficiencies for those who felt swamped. They decreased who needed to be at which meetings and recorded better notes for communicating decisions made in those meetings. And so on. These are the very essence of low-hanging fruit—still delicious but not such a struggle to obtain!

Let's look how your team might identify key areas to address and avoid a few pitfalls.

Identifying Your Organization's Unique, High-Impact Bandwidth Boosters

Once you've ascertained the urgency of bandwidth work in your community based on individual scores as well as scores on the energy, efficacy, and efficiency items, take a hard look at the organization items. Where are people in your community struggling? Again, this will help you narrow down which norms or policies need attention.

- I have enough work time and resources to handle my responsibilities.
- My workplace respects my personal life. I can "unplug" from the office after hours and on weekends.
- I have enough control over my work calendar that I can schedule my days in ways that allow me to be proactive rather than reactive.
- Multitasking, such as checking emails during meetings or calls, is discouraged by my workplace.
- My workplace supports checking emails only at set intervals during the day.
- All types of smartphone or computer usage while driving, including hands-free voice call meetings, are strongly discouraged by my workplace.
- Management where I work fosters a work environment that allows me to be effective.
- At work I am able to find blocks of time to concentrate without being interrupted when working on tasks that require focus.
- The meetings I attend are a good use of my time.
- I have time and energy for curiosity at work—pursuing new ideas, problems I'd like to solve, or experiments with creativity.
- The office atmosphere allows for building constructive relationships with colleagues.

Again, blameless discernment will help. What are the lowest scores? Then think through the following questions.

Identify factors that account for the current state of affairs. What rationalizations do leaders give? Teachers? In other words, think historically about how the norms or policies came to be or why people assume things can't be any other way. How might that inform a new way forward?

Consider individual responsibility and organizational responsibility. In particular, look for assumptions and excuses. For example, one school's policy of always getting back to parents before the end of the school day originated when parents could only leave phone messages. When leaders identified how the increased volume of emails, especially those arriving toward the end of the school day, meant that teachers couldn't honor the policy and leave even close to on time, they altered the policy.

Distinguish between equity and equality. Given school schedules, contracts, and staff responsibilities, some changes will help some learning community members more than others. Remember that equity and fairness do not always mean treating everyone the same. For example, a new norm might help everyone but the kindergarten teachers. While a "treat everyone the same" approach would dismiss such a norm as unfair, an equitable approach would implement this for the other 90 percent of the staff and find a different approach for the kindergarten teachers! Not treating everyone the same is the equitable approach in these situations.

Rely on your data. You can disaggregate the data to understand who is struggling most with bandwidth. This might unearth a current inequity, such as specialists having more families to interact with, or a policy having a disproportionate impact because of team meeting schedules.

Reset norms and policies while considering the restraints of your learning community. What do we mean by this? Let's look at the common low-scoring items to understand.

Everybody Laughs at Power Naps

Consider your learning community's scores for the following list of the items that, as mentioned in Chapter 2, in our research showed the lowest scores.

- I attend to emails at set times rather than constantly.
- I use power naps to clear my mind.
- I have regular meditation or yoga or other reflective practices.
- I avoid multitasking.
- I set aside uninterruptible blocks of time of at least 60 minutes to work on projects that require deep concentration.
- When I am driving, I don't text or talk on my phone.
- I have activities that allow me to relax my mind.
- I find time to follow my own creative pathways for learning, research, and problem solving.

We believe scores are low on these items because people now take for granted many unhealthy norms and practices. We need to back up and say, "Are these the norms we want? Where did they come from? Are they serving us?"

Let's start with power naps as an example of how you might roll out a new norm that on the surface seems crazy for schools. Did you just give a sarcastic snort? When we talk with schools about changing norms, someone always seems to quip, "Right, let's make a new norm about power naps." And everyone laughs at this crazy notion that teachers might nap during the school day.

However, even our military now advocates naps for solid, effective performance, according to *New York Times* reporter David Phillips (2020). What if there was a way to norm them in schools? And what if power naps turned out to be the low-hanging-fruit—the cheapest, most efficient way to increase everyone's bandwidth? How might you make it a new norm so that no one feels guilty when they nap and no one feels like those who nap are shirking? After all, they aren't. Go back to Chapter 9 for the solid evidence that if you need a nap, 20 minutes of shut-eye out of an hour of work time allows you to accomplish as much as if you try to power through and fight that mind-fogging fatigue. Plus, you'll have more EQ-boosting bandwidth.

So how might a school create a norm that encourages power naps? Try putting your creativity to use. Below are three strategies for exploring new norms for *any* bandwidth issue.

Use collective creativity. In a meeting, post the fact that "60 minutes of planning when tired = 20-minute nap + 40 minutes of planning."

Then, have staff work in small groups to discuss when they might fit in a quick nap at school while fulfilling all their responsibilities. Note that 15 minutes of snoozing before commuting home might decrease road rage and distracted driving and increase patience for those you love! Or what about just as people arrive? Those whose sleep was interrupted by small children might see the wisdom of a short nap before students arrive. What else is possible? A protein bar lunch to free up time occasionally? This same collective creativity can be used to find blocks of uninterrupted time to concentrate, avoid multitasking, and so on—whichever bandwidth issue needs solving.

Experiment. Have everyone commit to trying power naps over the course of a month. Have fun with it—put up a bulletin board somewhere for staff members to post stickers whenever they successfully nap (or perhaps they add a "Zzzz" with a marker). In a meeting, take time to reflect on whether power naps make a difference. If you're targeting blocks of uninterrupted time, make a thermometer as you would for fundraising with goal levels for hours of concentration. What other ways might you visibly celebrate progress?

Model. Have leadership and your bandwidth team be the first to nap—or hide somewhere to concentrate or take any other suggested action to improve bandwidth. Report out on what happens. Are you more energized, effective, efficient, and engaged? What happens to your emotional intelligence? Communicate this to the rest of the learning community, and remember that no one feels empowered for self-care unless leadership is modeling it.

> I recall my first year of teaching that when I took a walk around the school with a colleague during lunch, I felt guilty like I was "playing hooky." Now there is widespread acceptance when a teacher steps away from their desk for self-care. For instance, walking during your prep time outside or on the new track in the gymnasium is encouraged. Leaders have modeled this practice too, as I see them walking outside in the afternoon through my window in the classroom. I feel like there is a shared understanding that if we as teachers feel good, we can be better teachers for our students.
>
> —Alternative Learning Program Lead Teacher

As you try these strategies, make sure to give any new initiative enough time for people to develop the associated habits—look back at this chapter's Curiosity Creator on how long it takes to change habits. For example, were people able to develop capacity to power nap? And make sure that people move away from the attitude of "I didn't think it would work, so I didn't try it, and sure enough, it didn't work."

Try these three strategies—collective creativity, experimenting, modeling—to find time to concentrate, personalize mindfulness exercises, or explore better norms in other bandwidth areas. Look for the latitude to do things differently, experiment, and get out of habit and routine. Think different.

The Bandwidth Community Survey in Action

An elementary school chose to use our Brain Energy and Bandwidth Survey as the teacher leaders worked with administrators to change what they termed a "negative culture." Feedback from teachers as they moved back to in-person learning after the COVID-19 pandemic indicated that trust among staff had decreased; there were complaints that the administrators didn't realize the stress teachers had faced through the months of distance and hybrid learning.

Indeed, over two-thirds of the staff who took the survey reported a serious bandwidth deficit—a score of less than 60 on the individual items. Most believed that leadership only sometimes or seldom fostered an environment that let them be efficient. Yet three-fourths reported a good or high level of self-efficacy. In other words, they still felt they were accomplishing goals and found meaning and purpose in their work.

As Jane met with the leadership team, including teacher leaders, she asked them to first reflect with a partner on the learning community behaviors associated with each level of bandwidth. The groups all agreed that "mediocre" summed up the general feeling in the building, although one or two teams might be lower. However, they also agreed that the low individual scores meant that their school staff was in danger of losing ground on energy, passion, and control of time. "If some teachers are that low on bandwidth, their level of effectiveness just isn't sustainable, is it?" the principal pointed out.

The group then worked in the same pairs to consider the rest of the survey data, each pair focusing on a separate section of the survey. What were the lowest-scoring items? How might school norms or policies affect the individual items? Each group made "keep doing, start doing, stop doing" lists on flip chart paper to capture their thoughts.

For example, two low aggregate items were "I build my schedule to allow for meeting overruns and traffic delays" and "The in-person meetings I attend are a good use of my time." The group looking at "making time work for you" suggested several simple action steps, including

- Ending before-school professional development sessions 15 minutes before the start of classes.

- Holding before-school meetings only on Tuesdays, Wednesdays, or Thursdays.
- Starting walk-and-talk team meetings, taking notes via phone dictation.

The group that examined "focus through mental habits" noted that "I attend to emails at set times rather than constantly" was the school's second-lowest aggregate item. One easy action step they came up with was to ensure that the weekly email from the school principal, with key action items and announcements, could be sent at the same time every week—and on Thursday, not Friday, so that staff could allocate time to address action items rather than creating a bit of panic on Friday afternoons. Other action steps they proposed included

- Norming using "away messages" for emails, indicating the set times during which teachers would respond to them.
- Communicating to families why and when emails would be answered.
- Norming not answering emails from 5:00 p.m. to 8:00 a.m. to allow for personal time.
- Reducing the use of "reply all."

The other groups came up with many more suggestions. At the end of the session, the leadership commented on how many of these simple steps honored teacher needs and might thus begin to rebuild trust among staff.

A Final Thought

Think of using the survey as a gift to each member of your learning community. You're committed to improving norms and increasing their knowledge of how to use their brains. As you read through these comments from participants, ponder how your community might benefit.

> As a result of learning more about bandwidth, the leadership had great discussions about the "perceived" rules that some staff were following. We were able to address some issues that were draining staff by realizing we needed to improve our communications. Some families expected or wanted an immediate

answer to their email. Some teachers were then constantly checking email throughout the day and responding, which was taking time away from actual teaching. As we discussed this, we decided to make a template for staff to explain that emails will be answered during specific time frames. Everyone would receive a clear message and could then focus on their students.

—School International Baccalaureate Coordinator

Looking at the data for me was very helpful and informative. Reflection is always good, but what I appreciated the most was looking for the common good for our staff to help us move forward with all our mental health needs.

After reviewing the data, we were able to find common needs and find an action plan to move forward. Working with partners and discussing ways to move forward was extremely helpful. We were able to look at ideas from Jane's presentation and say, "Yes! This is exactly what we need. We can make this happen by. . . ." So many things that can be done are simple, easy to change, and have a "buy in" that works for both administration and staff.

—Teacher Leader

I learned that I could increase my bandwidth by making simplistic changes in my life. I can answer emails during a set time of the day. I can leave my school day behind and work school day hours. I can sleep with my phone in the other room. Most importantly, I need to take care of me. Eat healthy, get enough sleep, take power naps, and exercise.

—First Grade Teacher

After such a tricky, complex year, our conversations around bandwidth are particularly energizing for me, and they give me hope (and intention) about moving forward. I feel particularly excited about modeling self-care and voicing rest and balance to my team. If we are not caring for ourselves, we cannot show up as our best selves for our colleagues, students, and families. As a society where we value the hustle, exhaustion, and a never-ending to-do list, it is the brave thing to model rest, stillness, and gratitude. I am beyond excited to lean into this work. After all, we are all humans doing human work. To me, this is the most important kind of work. As school leaders, if we provide a space where all people can show up as our authentic, imperfect selves, great things can happen.

—EL Teacher and District EL Coordinator

Five Learning Community Leadership Bandwidth Booster Pathways

1. **Keep doing. Stop doing. Start doing.** One way to organize your data discussion is to make three lists:
   - Healthy norms and policies that are supporting good bandwidth (Keep Doing)
   - Unhealthy norms and policies that negatively impact individual bandwidth (Stop Doing)
   - Action steps we might take to support good bandwidth (Start Doing)
     Then prioritize at least items, and consider criteria such as impact and ease of implementation to choose your first action steps.
2. **Experiments.** In this chapter, we gave a few examples of how you might help people experiment with new actions to experience having more bandwidth. What other experiments might you engage in as a learning community? For example, what if every PLC team tried a walking meeting? What if everyone hands their cell phone to someone else for the duration of a meeting (we've facilitated this when working with groups on bandwidth, and the insights people have about their habits are impactful)? These experiments can become catalysts for change.
3. **Leadership modeling.** As mentioned above, leaders have a responsibility to model good bandwidth habits. Discuss and then act on ways you can make your own pathways to good bandwidth visible to others.

4. **Door signs.** Think of how some schools have everyone post a sign on their door like "I'm currently reading . . ." to encourage sustained, silent reading by students. How might you use this strategy to improve bandwidth? Remember that when we state our goals and why they're so important, we're far more likely to reach them.

5. **Measure.** Because we really only pay attention to what we measure, identify how you will measure progress on the action steps you take. You can always readminister the Brain Energy and Bandwidth Survey, but intermediate signs of progress can be encouraging and fun. What can you add to this list?

- Display a graph at staff meetings on how many teachers are leaving the building on time.
- Display *Zs* or other counters for who took power naps, got enough sleep, engaged in their chosen form of fitness, etc.
- Similar to a manufacturing sign counting the number of "days without a workplace accident," post a sign showing the number of "weeks where everyone got a period to concentrate deeply on a project."
- Display where teachers can add a mark indicating when they engage calmly with discipline.

Bandwidth Band Discussion Guide

1. What was the most important thing you learned for yourself as a leader/influencer as you worked with your learning community's Brain Energy and Bandwidth Survey results?

2. What was the most important thing you learned for the organization?

3. How will you know or what will you see if your organization is changing norms and policies that truly improve individual bandwidth *besides* just giving the survey again? Might some individual be aware of the overall pulse, perhaps a staff member people confide in? What would you see and hear in classrooms, hallways, or meetings if bandwidth is improving? How might student performance be affected if adults have more bandwidth? The more specific you are on what you look for, the more you'll be able to course-correct if necessary—and celebrate as progress is made!

Acknowledgments

We are both grateful to Greg Husczczo, PhD, who agreed to take on the data analysis for the Brain Energy and Bandwidth survey. He helped us structure and verify the survey so results corresponded to what we hoped to be measuring.

Jane: Thank you to Anita Rios, who in her role in leadership development at Minnesota State Colleges and Universities supported our first use of the "bandwidth quiz" with their aspiring leaders. And thank you to the leaders I coached who chose to use the early versions of the survey with their staffs: Renee Buchard at OXFAM, Marion Dalacker at Michael Foods, Katie Warren and Michael Kyle at St. Olaf College, Chad Schmidt in his work with Minnesota Learning Forward as well as his own learning community, my doctoral students at the University of St. Thomas, and other groups and schools around the world. Thank you to school leaders who attended the first workshop version of our work on bandwidth at Learning Forward back in 2017—we had such fun and you provided so many great examples of how learning communities might nurture better bandwidth in each member. And as always, thank you to my retired teacher husband, Brian, who makes sure I stay fueled, well connected, and in line with our priorities!

Ann: I would like to acknowledge the input and insights from teachers Natalie Ann Espe, Carly Pease, Cristine Czajka Conway, and Stu Pease. Our conversations discussing what it's like to teach, especially during the COVID-19 pandemic, were instrumental in understanding the challenges today's teachers face. I also appreciate the energizing conversations with my daughter, Chrissy Holm, who helped me stay motivated when I was procrastinating. Thank you to my son, Andrew Holm, who helped me form the mental habit of considering multiple perspectives before drawing any conclusions. I would also like to acknowledge friends and colleagues Joe Lynch and Mike Temple, who promoted the upcoming book on their podcasts. Likewise, I want to acknowledge the support from my best friend and patient listener Katherine Emmons, especially when I am spinning. Although he is not here anymore, I must acknowledge my late father, Andy Czajka, who wrote me a game-changing letter in high school, laying out how my life would be infinitely more satisfying if I used my talents and didn't play around in school! He was right! Finally, thank you to my mother, Norma Czajka, who gave me my stubborn grit, and to my husband, Mark Holm, who always sets a high bar for excellence.

Appendix:
Brain Energy and
Bandwidth Survey

To take the Brain Energy and Bandwidth Survey online and share it with other educators in your school, visit www.ascd.org/educator-bandwidth -survey.

Section I: Individual Bandwidth Components

Please provide a numerical answer for each question using the following scale: 0 (Almost Never), 1 (Seldom), 2 (Sometimes), 3 (Frequently), 4 (Almost Always)

1. **Balancing Priorities: Total _____**

    _____ I feel rested when I get up in the morning.

    _____ I have activities that allow me to relax my mind such as reading, listening to music, TV, or web surfing.

    _____ I make sure I take time for rest when I am ill.

    _____ After work, I still have plenty of patience for the most important people in my life.

    _____ I feel satisfied with the amount of time I spend with family and friends.

    _____ At important family and personal events or outings, I can keep my mind in the moment and let work issues go.

    _____ I take advantage of opportunities to maintain relationships with my coworkers.

2. Filtering Through Possibilities: Total ____

____ I monitor my internet surfing (researching information, images, travel arrangements, etc.) so that the time I spend is warranted by the decision I am making.

____ I have strategies to filter information that allow me to quickly choose among a few high-quality options and arrive at a satisfactory decision.

____ I can concentrate without being interrupted by worries about schedule/dieting/finances etc.

____ I avoid "decision fatigue" by automating some decisions (e.g., where I shop or what networking events I attend) to have more energy for others.

____ I find time to follow my own creative pathways for learning, research, and problem solving.

3. Focus Through Mental Habits: Total ____

____ I have regular meditation or yoga or journal or other reflective practices.

____ I avoid multitasking.

____ I use power naps to clear my mind.

____ I set aside uninterruptible blocks of time of at least 50 minutes to work on projects that require deep concentration.

____ I attend to emails at set times rather than constantly.

4. Fueling Our Brains: Total ____

____ I exercise regularly.

____ I make healthy food choices (e.g., balanced diet and my chosen indulgences in moderation).

____ I get enough sleep. Note: Indicators of insufficient sleep include being overly irritable or moody, craving junk food or caffeine, and struggling to stay alert.

____ I make sure I have access to water for staying hydrated.

5. **Staying Connected: Total** _____

   ____ I keep my social media use from interfering with what I need to accomplish.

   ____ I put my devices away when I'm engaged face to face with friends, family, or colleagues.

   ____ I know when I'm absentmindedly resorting to entertainment via my phone and put it down to engage with my surroundings.

   ____ My social media habits keep me connected without souring my mood.

   ____ When I am driving, I don't text or talk on my phone.

6. **Making Time Work for You: Total** _____

   ____ I manage multiple deadlines (i.e., no sudden realizations that I have overlooked something).

   ____ I build my schedule to allow for meeting overruns and traffic delays.

   ____ I am aware of the distracting dangers of email notifications, phone calls, and more, and I remove from my immediate environment those that interrupt my concentration.

   ____ I have strategies to delay important decisions until I can give them my full attention, especially at the end of long meetings or tiring days.

Total: Questions 1–6 _____

Section II: Individual Outcomes

7. **How would you rate the following over the past 60 days, with 0 as low and 4 as high?**

   ____ Your overall sense of energy

   ____ Your engagement level at work

   ____ Your sense of control over your schedule and workload

   ____ Your sense of self-efficacy—your ability to complete tasks and reach goals

   ____ Your ability to concentrate and get things done efficiently and effectively

   ____ Your ability to balance work life and personal life

_____ Your knowledge of how to use your brain energy both effectively and efficiently

_____ Your sense of meaning and purpose derived from your work responsibilities

Section III: Workplace Support

8. **Reflect on your experiences, thoughts, and feelings over the past 60 days and respond with the following scale: 0 (Almost Never), 1 (Seldom), 2 (Sometimes), 3 (Frequently), 4 (Almost Always)**

_____ I have enough work time and resources to handle my responsibilities.

_____ My workplace respects my personal life. I can "unplug" from the office after hours and on weekends.

_____ I have enough control over my work calendar that I can schedule my days in ways that allow me to be proactive rather than reactive.

_____ Multitasking, such as checking emails during meetings or calls, is discouraged by my workplace.

_____ My workplace supports checking emails only at set intervals during the day.

_____ All types of smartphone or computer usage while driving, including hands-free voice call meetings, are strongly discouraged by my workplace.

_____ Management where I work fosters a work environment that allows me to be effective.

_____ At work, I am able to find blocks of time to concentrate without being interrupted when working on tasks that require focus.

_____ The meetings I attend are a good use of my time.

_____ I have time and energy for curiosity at work—pursuing new ideas, problems I'd like to solve, or experiments with creativity.

_____ The office atmosphere allows for building constructive relationships with colleagues.

Notes

1. A. false. B. true. C. false. D. false. E. true.

2. Set 1: *C* is false. One in eight people believe life is long and easy in both regions of the world. The 12.5 percent who are more optimistic are significantly happier, do more volunteer work, vote more often, and donate more to charity (Tierney & Baumeister, 2019).

Set 2: *A* is false. Ansell (2015) reports that those who care for others, known as prosocial behavior, experience a buffering on the negative effects of stress on well-being.

References

Amichai-Hamburger, Y., & Etgar, S. (2016). Intimacy and smartphone multitasking—A new oxymoron? *Psychological Reports, 119*(3), 826–838.

Ansell, E. (2015, December 14). Helping others dampens the effects of everyday stress. *Clinical Psychological Science.* https://www.psychologicalscience.org/news/releases/helping-others-dampens-the-effects-of-everyday-stress.html

Arizmendi, T. G. (2011). Linking mechanisms: Emotional contagion, empathy, and imagery. *Psychoanalytic Psychology, 28*(3), 405–419.

Aschwanden, C. (2021, January 31). Forget about "magic immunity." Focus on sleep, exercise, diet, and cutting stress. *Washington Post.*

Bailey, C. (2016). *The productivity project: Proven ways to become more awesome.* Currency.

Bailey, C. (2018). *Hyperfocus: How to work less and achieve more.* Macmillan.

Baumeister, R. F., & Tierney, J. (2011) *Willpower: Rediscovering the greatest human strength.* Penguin.

Bernstein, L., Allen, M., Anton-Culver, H., Deapen, D., Horn-Ross, P. L., Peel, D., . . . & Ross, R. K. (2002). High breast cancer incidence rates among California teachers: Results from the California Teachers Study (United States). *Cancer causes & control, 13*(7), 625–635.

Black, S., & Allen, J. D. (2018). Part 5: Learning is a social act. *Reference Librarian, 59*(2), 76–91.

Busby, E. (2019, February 25). Teachers suffer more stress than other workers, study finds. *Independent.* https://www.independent.co.uk/news/education/education-news/teachers-stress-professionals-mental-health-workload-national-foundation-educational-research-a8795691.html

Carolus, A., Binder, J. F., Muench, R., Schmidt, C., Schneider, F., & Buglass, S. L. (2019). Smartphones as digital companions: Characterizing the relationship between users and their phones. *New Media & Society, 21*(4), 914–938.

Chamine, S. (2012). *Positive intelligence: Why only 20% of teams and individuals achieve their true potential and how you can achieve yours.* Greenleaf Book Group.

Christakis, N. A., & Fowler, J. H. (2007). The spread of obesity in a large social network over 32 years. *New England Journal of Medicine, 357*(4), 370–379.

Cipriano, C., & Brackett, M. (2020, April 7). Teachers are anxious and overwhelmed. They need SEL now more than ever. *EdSurge.* https://www.edsurge.com/news/2020-04-07-teachers-are-anxious-and-overwhelmed-they-need-sel-now-more-than-ever

Clear, J. (2014, June 10). How long does it actually take to form a new habit? (Backed by science). *Huffpost.* https://www.huffpost.com/entry/forming-new-habits_b_5104807

Collaborative for Academic, Social and Emotional Learning. (2021). SEL: What are the core competence areas and where are they promoted? CASEL. https://casel.org/sel-framework/

Corwin Visible Learning+. (n.d.). Global research database. www.visiblelearningmetax.com/Influences

Crowley, P., Madeleine, P., & Vuillerme, N. (2019). The effects of mobile phone use on walking: A dual task study. *BMC Research Notes, 12*(1), N.PAG.

Csikszentmihalyi, M. (2009). *Creativity: Flow and the psychology of discovery and invention.* Harper Perennial Press.

de Souza-Talarico, J. N., Marin, M. F., Sindi, S., & Lupien, S. J. (2011). Effects of stress hormones on the brain and cognition: Evidence from normal to pathological aging. *Dementia & Neuropsychologia, 5*(1), 8–16.

Deloitte. (2018). 2018 global mobile consumer survey: A new era in mobile continues. https://www2.deloitte.com/content/dam/Deloitte/us/Documents/technology-media-telecommunications/us-tmt-global-mobile-consumer-survey-exec-summary-2018.pdf

Doidge, N. (2007). *The brain that changes itself: Stories of personal triumph from the frontiers of brain science.* Penguin.

Gallate, J., Wong, C., Ellwood, S., Roring, R. W., & Snyder, A. (2012). Creative people use nonconscious processes to their advantage. *Creativity Research Journal, 24*(2/3).

Geher, G., & Wedberg, N. (2020). *Positive evolutionary psychology: Darwin's guide to living a richer life.* Oxford University Press.

Gifford, J. (2019). The rule of 52 and 17: It's random, but it ups your productivity. *The Muse.* https://www.themuse.com/advice/the-rule-of-52-and-17-its-random-but-it-ups-your-productivity.

Giunti, M., & Atkins, L. C. (2020). Plain language and the paradox of understanding and information availability. *Journal of Multidisciplinary Research (1947–2900), 12*(2), 41–56.

Glasner-Edwards, S. (2015). *The addiction recovery skills workbook: Changing addictive behaviors using CBT, mindfulness, and motivational interviewing techniques.* New Harbinger Publications.

Gollwitzer, P. M., & Brandstätter, V. (1997). Implementation intentions and effective goal pursuit. *Journal of Personality & Social Psychology, 73*(1), 186–199.

Goldstein, D., & Kroeger, O. (2013). *Creative you: Using your personality type to thrive.* Atria Books.

Gómez-Pinilla, F. (2008). Brain foods: The effects of nutrients on brain function. *Nature Reviews Neuroscience, 9*(7), 568–578.

Governors Highway Safety Association. (2020, February 27). New projection: 2019 pedestrian fatalities highest since 1988. https://www.ghsa.org/resources/news-releases/pedestrians20

Grant, A. (2016). *Originals: How non-conformists move the world.* Penguin.

Gwinn, A. (2019, December 12). Are your friends making you fat? *AARP.* https://www.aarp.org/health/healthy-living/info-2019/friends-influence-eating-habits.html

Hatfield, E., Cacioppo, J. T., & Rapson, R. L. (1993). Emotional contagion. *Current Directions in Psychological Science, 2*(3), 96–99.

Heath, C., & Heath, D. (2010). *Switch: How to change things when change is hard.* Broadway Books.

Hughes, V. (2013, July 31). The orphanage problem. *National Geographic.* www.nationalgeographic.com/science/phenomena/2013/07/31/the-orphanage-problem

Johnson, B. (2020). Polarity partnerships. www.polaritypartnerships.com

Judah, G., Gardner, B., & Aunger, R. (2013). Forming a flossing habit: An exploratory study of the psychological determinants of habit formation. *British Journal of Health Psychology, 18*(2), 338–353.

Jung, Y. H., Shin, N. Y., Jang, J. H., Lee, W. J., Lee, D., Choi, Y., . . ., & Kang, D. H. (2019). Relationships among stress, emotional intelligence, cognitive intelligence, and cytokines. *Medicine, 98*(18), e15345.

Juszczyk, D., & Gillison, F. (2018). Juicy June: A mass-participation snack-swap challenge—Results from a mixed methods feasibility study. *Pilot & Feasibility Studies, 4*(1), N.PAG.

Kaushal, N., & Rhodes, R. (2015). Exercise habit formation in new gym members: A longitudinal study. *Journal of Behavioral Medicine, 38*(4), 652–663.

Kelly, K. (2016). *The inevitable: Understanding the 12 technological forces that will shape our future.* Penguin.

Kise, J. A. G. (2019). *Holistic leadership, thriving schools: Twelve lenses to balance priorities and serve the whole student.* Solution Tree.

Klein, A. (2021). 1,500 decisions a day—at least: how teachers cope with a dizzying array of questions. *Education Week.* https://www.edweek.org/teaching-learning/1-500-decisions-a-day-at-least-how-teachers-cope-with-a-dizzying-array-of-questions/2021/12?utm_source=nl&utm_medium=eml&utm_campaign=tu&M=64239163&U=497400&UUID=c9828e369accc70611d0bcca8c74bc30

Kliemann, N., Vickerstaff, V., Croker, H., Johnson, F., Nazareth, I., & Beeken, R. (2017). The role of self-regulatory skills and automaticity on the effectiveness of a brief weight loss habit-based intervention: Secondary analysis of the 10 top tips randomised trial. *International Journal of Behavioral Nutrition & Physical Activity, 14*(1), 1–11.

Kovács, I., & Borcsa, M. (2017). The relationship between anxiety, somatic symptoms and hardiness in adolescence. *Romanian Journal of Applied Psychology, (19)2*, 42–49.

Lee, J. (2020, November 17). A neuropsychological exploration of zoom fatigue. *Psychiatric Times.* https://www.psychiatrictimes.com/view/psychological-exploration-zoom-fatigue

Leiberman, M. (2013). *Social: Why our brains are wired to connect.* Crown.

Lewis, M. (2012, September 11). Obama's way. *Vanity Fair.* https://www.vanityfair.com/news/2012/10/michael-lewis-profile-barack-obama

Lustig, R. H. (2017). *The hacking of the American mind: The science behind the corporate takeover of our bodies and brains.* Avery.

Maddi, S. R. (2005). On hardiness and other pathways to resilience. *American Psychologist, 60*(3), 261–262.

Maltz, M. (1960). *Psycho-cybernetics: A new way to get more living out of life.* Simon & Schuster.

Mark, G., Wang, Y., & Niiya, M. (2014). Stress and multitasking in everyday college life: An empirical study of online activity. *Proceedings of the SIGCHI Conference on Human Factors in Computing Systems,* 41–50.

McGonigal, K. (2011). *The willpower instinct: How self-control works, why it matters, and what you can do to get more of it.* Penguin.

McGonigal, K. (2013). How to make stress your friend. TED. https://www.ted.com/talks/kelly_mcgonigal_how_to_make_stress_your_friend#t-490046

McKeough, T. (2020, April 20). The small space workout challenge. *New York Times.* https://www.nytimes.com/2020/04/20/realestate/home-workout-small-space.html

McKeown, G. (2014). *Essentialism: The disciplined pursuit of less.* Crown Business.

Medina, J. (2014). *Brain rules: 12 principles for surviving and thriving at work, home and school.* Updated and expanded edition. Pear Press.

Mehta, R., Rui, J. Z., & Cheerma, A. (2012). Is noise always bad? Exploring the effects of ambient noise on creative cognition. *Journal of Consumer Research, 39*(4), 784–799.

Melumad, S., & Pham, M. T. (2020). The smartphone as a pacifying technology. *Journal of Consumer Research, 47*(2), 2–19.

Misra, S., Cheng, L., Genevie, J., & Yuan, M. (2014, July). The iPhone effect: The quality of in-person social interactions in the presence of mobile devices. *Environment and Behavior, 48*(2), 275–298.

Moss, M. (2013, February 20). The extraordinary science of addictive junk food. *New York Times.* https://www.nytimes.com/2013/02/24/magazine/the-extraordinary-science-of-junk-food.html

Mullainathan, S., & Shafir, E. (2013). *Scarcity: Why having too little means so much.* Times Books.

Multi-Health Systems. (2011). EQi-2.0 model of emotional intelligence.

Nardi, D. (2011). *The neuroscience of personality.* Radiance House.

National Library of Medicine. (2012). Tips for getting a good night's sleep. *NIH Medline Plus.* https://magazine.medlineplus.gov/pdf/MLP_Summer2012web.pdf

Newman, M. E. J. (2005). Power laws, Pareto distributions, and Zipf's law. *Contemporary Physics, 46*(5): 323–351.

Noddings, N. (2013). Standardized curriculum and loss of creativity. *Theory into Practice, 52*(3), 210–215.

Odell, J. (2019). *How to do nothing.* Melville House.

Pang, A. S. (2016). *Rest: Why you get more done when you work less.* Basic Books.

Peck, M. S. (1978). *The road less traveled: A new psychology of love, traditional values and spiritual growth.* Touchstone.

Perrin, A., & Kumar, M. (2019, July 25). Three-in-ten U.S. adults say they are"almost constantly" online. Pew Research Center. https://www.pewresearch.org/fact-tank/2019/07/25/americans-going-online-almost-constantly/

Phillips, D. (2020). The army rolls out a new weapon: Strategic naps. *New York Times.* https://www.nytimes.com/2020/10/01/us/army-naps.html

Powdthavee, N. (2008). Putting a price tag on friends, relatives, and neighbours: Using surveys of life satisfaction to value social relationships. *Journal of Socio-economics, 37*(4), 1459–1480.

Price, C. (2018). *How to break up with your phone: The 30-day plan to take back your life.* Ten Speed Press.

Pross, N. (2017). Effects of dehydration on brain functioning: A life-span perspective. *Annals of Nutrition & Metabolism, 70,* 30–36.

Radesky, J. S. (2020). Smartphones and children: Relationships, regulation, and reasoning. *CyberPsychology, Behavior & Social Networking, 23*(6), 361–362.

Radesky, J. S., Kistin, C., Eisenberg, S., Gross, J., Block, G., Zuckerman, B., & Silverstein, M. (2016). Parent perspectives on their mobile technology use: The excitement and exhaustion of parenting while connected. *Journal of Developmental & Behavioral Pediatrics, 37*(9), 694–701.

Rinkevich, J. (2011). Creative teaching: Why it matters and where to begin. *Clearing House, 84*(5), 219–223.

Ratey, J. (2013). *Spark: The revolutionary new science of exercise and the brain.* Little, Brown.

Reynolds, G. (2020, December 2). 11 minutes of exercise a day may help counter the effects of sitting. *New York Times.* https://www.nytimes.com/2020/12/02/well/move/exercise-sitting-longevity.html

Robson, D. (2019). *The intelligence trap: Why smart people make dumb mistakes.* Norton.

Sandberg, S. (2013). *Lean in: Women, work and the will to lead.* Knopf.

Schelb, E. (2020). Nutritional psychiatry: Your brain on food. *Harvard Health Publishing.* https://www.health.harvard.edu/blog/nutritional-psychiatry-your-brain-on-food-201511168626

Schwartz, B. (2004). *The paradox of choice: Why less is more.* Harper Books.

Schwartz, T. (2011). *The way we're working isn't working.* Free Press.

Simon, H. A. (1947). *Administrative behavior: A study of decision-making processes in administrative organization* (1st ed.). Macmillan.

Skakon, J., Nielsen, K., Borg, V., & Guzman, J. (2010). Are leaders' well-being, behaviours and style associated with the affective well-being of their employees? A systematic review of three decades of research. *Work Stress, 24,* 107–139.

Smart, A. (2013). *Auto-pilot: The art and success of doing nothing.* OR Books.

Steiner-Adair, C., & Barker, T. H. (2013). *The big disconnect: Protecting childhood and family relationships in the digital age.* Harper.

Stickgold, R. (2009). *The neuroscience of sleep.* Academic Press.

Stuckey, H. L., & Nobel, J. (2010). The connection between art, healing, and public health: A review of current literature. *American Journal of Public Health, 100*(2), 254–263.

Sun, J., & Leithwood, K. (2015). Leadership effects on student learning mediated by teacher emotions. *Societies, 5,* 566–582.

Tanil, C. T., & Yong, M. H. (2020). Mobile phones: The effect of its presence on learning and memory. *PLoS ONE, 15*(8), 1–12.

Tierney, J., & Baumeister, R. (2019). *The power of bad: How the negativity effect rules us and how we can rule it.* Penguin.

United States Department of Agriculture. (n.d.). What you should know about popular diets. Nutrition.gov. https://www.nutrition.gov/topics/healthy-living-and-weight/what-you-should-know-about-popular-diets

United States Department of Veterans Affairs. (n.d.). Mindful eating. https://www.move.va.gov/docs/NewHandouts/BehavioralHealth/B11_MindfulEating.pdf

Walker, M. (2017). *Why we sleep: Unlocking the powers of sleep and dreams.* Scribner.

Wegner, D. M. (1989). *White bears and other unwanted thoughts: Suppression, obsession, and the psychology of mental control.* Viking Adult.

Weir, K. (2020b, April). Nurtured by nature. *Monitor on Psychology, 51*(3). http://www.apa.org/monitor/2020/04/nurtured-nature

Wheatley, M., & Kellner-Rogers, M. (1999, June). What do we measure and why? Questions about the uses of measurement. *Journal for Strategic Performance Measurement.*

Wiedemann, A. U., Gardner, B., Knoll, N., & Burkert, S. (2014). Intrinsic rewards, fruit and vegetable consumption, and habit strength: A three-wave study testing the associative-cybernetic model. *Applied Psychology: Health and Well-Being, 6,* 119–134.

Wise, R. A. (1996). Addictive drugs and brain stimulation reward. *Annual Review of Neuroscience, 19,* 319–340.

Wolf, M. (2018). *Reader, come home: The reading brain in a digital world.* Harper.

Zahariades, D. (2015). *The Pomodoro technique: A 10-step action plan for increasing your productivity* (1st electronic ed.). Author.

Zenger, J., & Folkman, J. (2009). *The extraordinary leader: Turning good managers into great leaders.* McGraw-Hill.

Zomorodi, M. (2017). *Bored and brilliant: Rediscovering the lost art of spacing out.* St. Martin's Press.

Index

The letter *f* following a page locator denotes a figure.

About the Authors

Jane A. G. Kise, EdD, CPQC, founder of Differentiated Coaching Associates, has worked as a consultant for 30 years, specializing in executive and instructional coaching and professional development. She is also the author or coauthor of over 25 books, including *Doable Differentiation; Holistic Leadership, Thriving Schools; Differentiated Coaching: A Framework for Helping Teachers Change;* and *Creating a Coaching Culture for Professional Learning Communities.* She holds an MBA in finance from the Carlson School of Management and a doctorate in educational leadership from the University of St. Thomas, where she is an adjunct professor for the doctoral program.

Kise is also a certified practitioner with Polarity Assessments, the Hogan Assessments, the EQi-2.0 and 360 instruments, the Pearman Personality Integrator, and other feedback tools. She is a certified Positive Intelligence Coach specializing in helping educators build mental fitness capacity and hardiness.

Kise has worked with education organizations and businesses across the United States and in Saudi Arabia, Europe, Australia, and New Zealand. Current and past clients include public and private schools, Minnesota State Colleges and Universities, NASA, and the Minnesota Department of Education. She is a frequent keynoter and workshop speaker and has presented at Learning Forward, ASCD, NCTM, NCSM, World Futures, and Association for Psychological Type conferences.

Ann C. Holm, MS, PCC, CPQC, is a professional certified coach specializing in executive leadership and personal development. She is an MBTI Master Practitioner and is known as a thought leader in integrating psychological type theory with other coaching models, including Emotional Intelligence, Positive Intelligence, and Polarity Thinking, where she holds certifications. In addition, Holm has 25 years of experience in applied brain science as a speech-language pathologist specializing in stroke and brain injury rehabilitation. She is a frequent podcast guest and is the author of numerous articles and blogs.

Ann holds a bachelor's degree in psychology, speech, and hearing and a master's degree in speech-language pathology from the University of Michigan, along with a certificate in organizational development from the University of Minnesota. She received coach training from the Coaches Training Institute and is certified by the International Coaching Federation. Past clients include schools ranging from pre-K to post-secondary, small business owners, and teams in the logistics industry.

Related ASCD Resources

At the time of publication, the following resources were available (ASCD stock numbers in parentheses).

Print Products

The Burnout Cure: Learning to Love Teaching Again by Chase Mielke (#119004)

Manage Your Time or Time Will Manage You: Strategies That Work from an Educator Who's Been There by PJ Caposey (#119005)

Mindfulness in the Classroom: Strategies for Promoting Concentration, Compassion, and Calm by Thomas Armstrong (#120018)

The Minimalist Teacher by Tamera Musiowsky-Borneman and C. Y. Arnold (#121058)

Overcoming Educator Burnout (Quick Reference Guide) by Chase Mielke (#QRG123016)

Teach, Reflect, Learn: Building Your Capacity for Success in the Classroom by Pete Hall and Alisa Simeral (#115040)

The Teacher 50: Critical Questions for Inspiring Classroom Excellence by Baruti Kafele (#117009)

For up-to-date information about ASCD resources, go to **www.ascd.org**. You can search the complete archives of *Educational Leadership* at **www.ascd.org/el**.

ASCD myTeachSource®

Download resources from a professional learning platform with hundreds of research-based best practices and tools for your classroom at http://myteachsource.ascd.org

For more information, send an email to member@ascd.org; call 1-800-933-2723 or 703-578-9600; send a fax to 703-575-5400; or write to Information Services, ASCD, 2800 Shirlington Rd., Ste. 1001, Arlington, VA 22206 USA.

WHOLE CHILD
TENETS

THE WHOLE CHILD

The ASCD Whole Child approach is an effort to transition from a focus on narrowly defined academic achievement to one that promotes the long-term development and success of all children. Through this approach, ASCD supports educators, families, community members, and policymakers as they move from a vision about educating the whole child to sustainable, collaborative actions.

Educator Bandwidth relates to the **supported** tenet.

For more about the ASCD Whole Child approach, visit www.ascd.org/wholechild.

1 HEALTHY
Each student enters school healthy and learns about and practices a healthy lifestyle.

2 SAFE
Each student learns in an environment that is physically and emotionally safe for students and adults.

3 ENGAGED
Each student is actively engaged in learning and is connected to the school and broader community.

4 SUPPORTED
Each student has access to personalized learning and is supported by qualified, caring adults.

5 CHALLENGED
Each student is challenged academically and prepared for success in college or further study and for employment and participation in a global environment.